Joel Moody

The Song of Kansas and Other Poems

Joel Moody

The Song of Kansas and Other Poems

ISBN/EAN: 9783744714631

Printed in Europe, USA, Canada, Australia, Japan

Cover: Foto ©Thomas Meinert / pixelio.de

More available books at **www.hansebooks.com**

The Song of Kansas

and

Other Poems.

BY JOEL MOODY.

"There is no history so true as the poetic."
—*Marcella Howland.*

TOPEKA, KANSAS:
GEO. W. CRANE & CO.,
1890.

PREFACE.

EACH of these poems was written for a special purpose — to commemorate some fact or event in my own life. *The Song of Kansas* is a tribute to the State in which I have lived nearly thirty-two years. My life is a part of its history. I wrote the "Song" for my children, who were born in Kansas, and desired to know something of the early history of their State. For this purpose I have added ample notes.

The other poems connect me with things and persons, about which or to whom they were written, and thus they also are a part of my life. There has been of late a personal demand on me for their publication. I send them forth, not for profit or fame, but simply as messages of Patriotism, of Friendship, and Love.

THE AUTHOR.

THE MAPLES:
MOUND CITY, KANSAS,
September 1, 1890.

CONTENTS.

	PAGE.
PREFACE	v
CONTENTS	vii
THE SONG OF KANSAS	1
Introduction	3

I.
Coronado's March through the Plains in the Year 1541	5
The March	5

II.
The Advent of Columbia and the Natal Song of Kansas	15
Columbia	17
The Natal Hour	19

III.
The Struggle in Kansas with Freedom against the Great Hydra—American Slavery	21
Pardee Butler	25
Charles W. Dow	25
William Phillips	25
Thomas W. Barber	26
Andrew H. Reeder	27
The Invasion	28
Lawrence	28
Freedom's Champion	32
Liberty and John Brown	32
Col. John W. Geary	41
Linn	42
Osawanda	43
John Brown	75
The Civil War	78

Contents.

THE SONG OF KANSAS—Continued:

IV.

	PAGE.
Kansas in the Reign of Peace	80
Peace	80
The State	81
The Home	82
The Early Pioneer	85
The Prairie Fire	86
The Heroes	89
Commerce	88
The Flag	89
History's Wisdom	91
The Sunflower	93
The Patriot's Love	93
MISCELLANEOUS POEMS	95
The Prayer upon the Wall	97
Dawn	101
The Tear	102
Life	103
The Last Roll	104
University of Michigan: Threnody	107
Old Captain Sumpter	115
The Guest at Home	120
The Sawmill of the Gods	121
Looking Backward	124
A Young Lady's Holocaust	128
The Child of Fate	129
A Scotch Song: "Stormy Weather"	130
A German Drinking Song	131
"Exlmpt"	133
The Loaned Book	134
Alone	135
The Enchanted Garden	136
Silver Threads	137
What is the World to Me?	138
"The Maples"	140
HISTORIC NOTES	143

The Song of Kansas.

INTRODUCTION.

I STRIKE the chord of the enchanted shell
To Clio given, whose soft strains lingering dwell
With him who makes the ancient thing his joy,
And grateful is, those strains his steps decoy:—
With him who strays by ivy-mantled wall
And hears the trembling voice of Ages call:—
With him who in some dark abode or wild
Finds the first footprints of rude Nature's child,
With kalends numbered from the oldest page
And cut in sullen stone moss-grown with age:—
With him who dares to ride the endless main,
To tread the mountain tops and pathless plain,
Or to explore a world whose people eld
No page had known or civil eye beheld;
Or where within these ancient realms new forms
Arise, where civil life is built, where warms
The patriot heart, and in the fireside blaze
We find the old expiring as we gaze.
Fondly with the blue-eyed Muse I dwell,— she
Who haunts the restless realms of *History*.

The Song of Kansas.

I.

CORONADO'S MARCH THROUGH THE PLAINS IN THE YEAR 1541.

THE MARCH.

It was when pious, proud and bold
   Carlos the Fifth reigned king of Spain,
   Old chevaliers, with worldly gain
   Imbued, crossed the mighty main
To plant the cross, and search for gold.

Of valor, who shall question that?
   Each one a knight, had kissed the hand
   Of lady love, and sworn to stand
   By Honor's sword in foreign land,—
Swore by the spurs, and tipped the hat.

And thus stout men, and brave and true,
   Skilled in the art of war, and lore
   Of sea,— toward setting sun they bore,
   While Coronado, far from shore,
Waved his dear land a long adieu.

Thus, while King Charles did tell his beads
    And tinker at his clocks, there came,
    The highest on the roll of fame;
    The choicest chiefs,[1] in Honor's name,—
Valiant they came for valiant deeds,

To the great land of ancient mines,—
    To kingly Montezuma's home,—
    Through cities old and gray to roam,—
    To that rich realm in weirdly tome
Foretold by astrologic signs.

From the trackless path of the wide
    Sea came, to take the path on land
    Of many an Indian band;—
    Perchance to find and shake the hand
Of lost Nuñez, and him provide.[2]

And soon in part their hopes fulfilled;—
    The Spaniard lost on land and sea
    Cabeça came, and told in free
    And easy tale the story he
Had heard of men profoundly skilled

In all the arts of peace and war,—
    That he had traveled over plains
    Of weary sand, where kindly rains
    Had never come,—and mountain chains
Whose peaks, high capped in snows afar,

The Song of Kansas.

Were filled with gold; and that they stand
    Like sentinels to show the way
    To cities gemmed like some bright spray;
    And at their feet outspread did lay
Bounteous pastures, and fruitful land.

Heralder of a mighty state!
    Whose soil thy own brave feet have trod,
    Whose hand first waved the potent rod
    Of empire o'er her emerald sod,
Cabeça, first among the great!

Now, Coronado must adventure —
    He is a chosen child of Fate;
    His name must stand among the great, —
    Undaunted he of scorn or hate,
His star did not arise for censure.

On to Rio Colorado!
    Mark the dim trail which Diaz took!
    Search the land Alarçon forsook!
    Plant there the cross and Holy Book!
Then on again with Alvarado,

To rare old cities of the hills
    Held fast within their lap of earth,
    Whose history and ancient birth
    Forestalls the years; whose golden worth
The multitude with wonder fills! [3]

Weary and worn, those sturdy sons
   Of Spain marched on through torrid heat
   And stifling sands, at last to meet,
   Not hopes fulfilled, nor waters sweet
To taste, nor wealth in hoarded tons

To harvest in like golden sheaves;
   But savage men with filthy wives,
   And homes of mud for weirdly lives. [4]
   Then blasted hopes unsheathed the knives,
And Pueblos fell like Autumn leaves.

Then on old Zuñi's heights was woe:—
   Where once was freedom now the walled
   Fortress shuts in a race enthralled;—
   And where in peace and joy they called
Upon their gods, a foreign foe

Has turned to mockery their prayers.
   Then, ancient head and saint of years,
   Downcast, trembling and sick with fears,
   Implores the Hidden Power in tears
For one to save his race, who dares

To give his life that men may live:—
   And though the hand of Heaven be slow,
   The prayer unanswered does not go.
   A life is asked — no promised bow
In sky, or hand of brave to give,

But *him* who can fond hopes beguile;—
Who can with sly and studied art
Pluck every fear from his stout heart;—
Who can from home and world depart,
While Death wafts up to heaven his smile.

Such man was found. Nor do the years
Pass o'er a race of men or age,
In this old world's story, when rage
Of lust blots fair History's page,
Without some man whom time endears,

As the great savior of his race,
To come and offer up his life.
Not such as told of mythic strife
In ancient lore, or story rife
With deeds that do their gods disgrace;

Nor mighty one among the stars,
In Vedic poem sung; nor vast
Old giant of the earth, to cast
The weighty spear, and then at last
Forsake mankind, like bloody Mars;

But came then forth a man inspired
With holy, grand, immortal sense
Of love, which goes like sweet incense
Up to heaven, and is recompense
Alone for all of life required. [5]

In pity, then, this fable told
   The savage sage to save his race:
   That far away some hallow'd place
   Was known to him, where the white-face
Doth dwell and dress in silks and gold;

And that they eat from golden plates,
   With silver spoons and forks and knives;
   That fairies live with men as wives;
   That mankind live enchanted lives,
Where want comes not nor strifes nor hates;

That he will lead o'er hills and dells,
   To that fair land where cities old
   Are filled with tons of wealth untold;
   To where a king is clad in gold,
And sleeps 'neath trees with golden bells.

Brave savage guide! his story told,
   Dupes Coronado, and his train
   Of idol worshipers. In vain
   Shall death appall; he shall be slain,
And save mankind, like gods of old.

Then brought he forth the pipe of peace,
   And lit the sacred fire, and said:
   "This pipe I smoke, that our brave dead,
   Whose souls move round the mountain red
May come and give our woes release.

The Song of Kansas.

"Now will you go to old Quivira;
  To that fair land of our red pipe,[6]
  Where you may reap your harvest ripe
  Of brilliant hopes, and joyous wipe
All care away; where rests the weary?"

"I go," quoth he, "to clutch the spoil."
  And thus the pious fable wrought
  Into the fancies of his thought,
  And led him on, till he was taught
The solid facts of Kansas soil.

O'er the vast plains, upon the trail[7]
  Of old commercial bands, who bring
  The northern fur, for the bright wing
  Of tropic bird, they go wandering;
Far from their stores or friendly sail.

Through herds of buffalo,[8] who came
  With savage look and shaggy mane,
  To question why this warlike train
  Should here molest their ancient reign;
By whose command, and in what name.

Prophets they came, to tell these savage
  Monarchs of the grassy fields
  That the hard hand of Time, that wields
  The destiny of worlds, and shields
A race of men though born to ravage,

Now soon shall strike, and savage beast
    And savage man shall hear their doom:
    Give way! stand back! pass off! give room
    To the weird sisters of the *Loom!*
Hail! mighty Genius of the East.

Thus to Kansas Coronado came,
    With pious Turco for his guide;
    O'er blinding sands and rivers wide;
    Through valleys gay and rich they ride;
And find, not Fortune fair, — but Fame.

"Bring forth my Indian guide," quoth he;
    "Where is thy shining gold? Now tell!
    Shake mute thy head? Here goes to hell
    Thy soul!"— and the firm savage fell,
The first fruits of the golden tree. [9]

Thus the host of Coronado
    Entered on the plains of Kansas, —
    Thus they made the first advances,
    Not to possess her fields and ranches,
But to grasp a golden shadow.

Nor was the kingdom that he sought
    Filled with wisdom's storied page;
    Nor ruled by hoary-headed sage;—
    Here was no land to quench the rage
Of fancies that his brain had wrought.

He stopped far short of that famed land,
  Which princely Madoc's children name;
  Whose beauteous face and manly frame
  Bespoke a race of Cimric fame;
Long lost on the Atlantic strand.[10]

He found Quivira wild and fair,
  Nature's rude child; yet in her face
  Might see the vision of a race
  That, clasped within her fond embrace,
Should conquer earth, and sky, and air.

His was the life and his the era,
  When Fancy pictured Fancy's child;—
  A land where Summer, soft and mild,
  Cast flowers upon the Year, and smiled
To thus bedeck her fair Quivira.

Here on the banks of dark Missouri[11]
  The peaceful country found, but here
  For unrequited toil paid dear;
  The golden tree found not, nor tear
From savage eye, for savage story.

Here stayed his course, and waved the rod
  Of empire over Kansas, young
  And fair; and the dear cross where hung
  The Christ was raised, and hymn was sung,
In honor of his race and God.

His hopes a prophecy fulfilled, —
    The vision that he saw is ours, —
    Ours the gift of heavenly powers, —
    A golden land of fruits and flowers, —
And deeds which have the ages thrilled.

Then backward Coronado bent
    His course; sadly, slowly, unwept,
    He went. Here savage Virtue kept
    Her reign, and here fair Pallas [1] [2] slept
In peace, till dawned a great event.

II.

THE ADVENT OF COLUMBIA AND THE NATAL SONG OF KANSAS.

THREE hundred times and twelve, the great
   Pendulum which measures on its arc
   Both space and time, and there the dark
   Mysteries of passing years doth mark,
Ticked out the coming of a state.

And in those years what change has come!
   New empires rise while others die,—
   Cities of old in ruins lie,—
   And the new fret the vaulted sky,
With battlement and spacious dome.

And Europe's map, drawn in the face
   Of deadly War, on bloody field,
   Now sadly changed by those who wield
   The diplomatic axe, and shield
The conquering heroes of the race.

As with a wizard's touch old Spain
   Transformed; her knighthood gone, her star
   Of glory set at Trafalgar;—
   And yet fair Kansas, from afar,
Recalls the story of her reign.

The Song of Kansas.

Then came fair Science to indite
   Her hymn,—who with her hammer knocks
   High truths from out the solid rocks,
   And deftly cuts from Kansas blocks,
Grander than Cnidian Aphrodite.

She holds within her mystic hand
   The potent rod which doth unarm
   The mighty Jove,—she doth alarm
   The thunderer on his throne, and charm
His lightnings with her magic wand.

She hath disrobed the ancient myth,—
   Tracked home the planets and the suns,—
   Measured and weighed the minor ones:
   Now dusts her scales of sundry tons,
And then the atoms weighs therewith.

She doth invade old Neptune's realm,—
   Brings from his depths the hidden lore,—
   Speaks through his waves from shore to shore,
   And sets the trident that he bore,
On every sailor's prow and helm.

Cities unearthed stand forth and tell
   Old tales. To sight comes back the place
   Where Virgil sat,—and buried mace
   Of high old courts,—and Troy's proud race
Appears again, where Priam fell.

The Song of Kansas.

Now the firm hand is laid on ghost
That haunts Arcadia's ancient shades,—
The veil is torn away, and fades
Upon our sight the phantom maids,
And gods, which the old classics boast.

From time's great depths, dark India speaks
A wisdom by the priests of old,—
And gods appear in mystic mold,
Fair, lotus-eyed, in snaky fold,
Or sit in snows on mountain peaks.

Great Egypt, mistress of the Nile,
In hieroglyphic lore appears,—
Land of dark Memnon, and quaint seers,
And mystic rites; the sullen tears
Of Time make havoc of thy smile.

COLUMBIA.

Earth kissed the heaven, and then gave birth
To Tethys fair, whose soul on wings
Of fruitful love arose,—then springs
Immortal Doris forth, who brings
To manhood mighty sons of earth.

From these Columbia[13] comes forth,
A nereid of the sea, where old
Oceanus keeps his watery fold,—
She comes with hair like floating gold,—
Star-gemmed her robe,— of priceless worth

The Song of Kansas.

Her band; and wiping from her head
   The slimy wrongs which Ocean kept,
   And blinding tears sad Misery wept;
   Then on the surf-beat shore she stept,
And held aloft her hand, and said:

"From north to south, from east to west,
   To Truth and Liberty this land
   I dedicate; and here shall stand
   And live the right; here Law's command
Shall reign, and here mankind be blest.

"Here soon shall rise the dazzling sun,
   That gilds the shield of Liberty;—
   Sweet Virtue here shall honored be,—
   Here shall I plant the fruitful tree;
Here give to earth a Washington.

"Here shall I raise the starry flag,
   Now my encircling drapery,
   And on its ample folds shall be
   A constellation of the free.
Upon the highest mountain crag,

"And in the lowest vale or moat,—
   Upon the lakes and mighty streams
   On gulf and ocean's surge, its beams
   Shall fall on earth like angels' dreams,—
Here shall my proud flag freely float.

"And as the coming time advances,
  There shall upon this flag appear
  A central star; holy and clear
  Its light shall shine, and be more dear
To me than all,—that star is Kansas.

"Kansas the name—¹⁴ child of the wind
  That sweeps her grassy fields, and brings
  The storm upon his fretful wings,
  Or on the cyclone rides, and flings
The torn and scattered wreck behind.

"But ere that time shall come the flail
  Of Truth will fall upon this land,
  Harder than stroke of Titan's hand;
  The golden grain, by Heaven's command,
Is thrashed, and winnowed in the gale."

Thus said, the goddess flung her robe
  Upon the breeze, and took her flight
  From the Atlantic shore; her bright
  Path a blazing meteor's light,
With heavenly train, shone round the globe.

THE NATAL HOUR.

Decorate the Thirtieth of May! ¹⁵
  Shall we now the great act deplore
  Which gave us Kansas!—nevermore.
  She was called fresh from the dark shore
Of Time; she came; hail mighty day!

The Song of Kansas.

All hail! Kansas this day was born;
   Not full-fledged and armed, like fair
   Minerva from the matted hair
   Of Jove, to wing her flight in air,
And chant "*Ad astra*" to the morn;

But in the dark and sullen storm
   Of civil strife; like one without
   A friend or home; and tossed about
   Forlorn, and mocked by the rude shout
Of ruffian bands in demon's form.

Sweet Kansas of the fragrant plain!
   Thy natal hour shall mark a day
   Wreathed in flowery love; whose bright ray
   Shall gild the world, and whose sweet lay
Shall charm like some Æolian strain.

III.

THE STRUGGLE IN KANSAS WITH FREEDOM AGAINST THE GREAT HYDRA—AMERICAN SLAVERY.

AND now we turn the sable leaf
  Of that great book where Time records
  The wrongs, the strifes, the bitter words,
  Where Vice with Error's heart accords,
And read the story of our grief.

Quaff then the darker drink, brought fresh
  From Lethe's stream; for sure I am
  That when this world's great book you scan,
  No darker deeds are found, where man
Against mankind in living flesh

Has waged the wrong. Quaff and forget,
  That e'er the issue could be made,
  That ever promise had been laid,
  That ever human tongue had said,
Where man his brother man has met,

That slavery is right.[16] Here then
  The issue came, and war on earth:
  Shall Kansas from her hallow'd birth
  Be free or slave? Proclaim it forth,
And heaven and hell attend on men.

Slavery, like the great Python
    Apollo slew;—bred in the slime
    Of earth;—whose birth was the first crime
    Against mankind, and that sublime
Iniquity of hell to dethrone

The rights of man, now crawling winds
    Herein in slimy, snaky fold:
    Or like the dragon great of old,
    On Thebes' rich plain in story told,
Great Cadmus slew, and wond'rous finds

That from his teeth sown in the earth,
    A race of men comes forth from clods,
    For civil strife; and whom the gods
    Turned man to man, barring all odds,
Against his equal man by birth.

Python and dragon both, with fierce
    And bloody mouth, crawling it came;—
    Eyes that shot forth a burning flame
    Glared round for prey; and naught could tame
The gloated beast of hell, nor pierce

Its flinty scales, till it had fed
    And fattened on the blood and flesh
    Of Freedom's sons. This past, then fresh
    From ample meal the vengeful mesh
He slipped, and wounded, writhing fled.

The Song of Kansas.

But e'er that time let me recall,
   And briefly note, some deeds of crime,—
   Some deeds of valor won, sublime
   To stand throughout recorded time,—
Or passing note how heroes fall.

And Slavery's banner now unfurled
   Dark on the breeze of Kansas floats.
   Strange flag! on which foul Treason dotes;
   Whereon is writ: "Missouri votes
On Kansas soil, or bursts a world!"

Classical in the third degree!
   But what does Slavery care? her flag
   Floats not o'er classic halls; her rag
   Was made in Freedom's blood to drag,
And blazon forth iniquity.

And this strange flag herein they send,
   Painted in black, with threats of war,
   And words of hell,—and from afar
   Comes the red flag with its lone star,
And the ruffian to defend.

Then Slavery's champions these words
   Proclaim: "Come direful War and whet
   Thy sword; and let no freeman set
   His foot on Kansas soil,—[17] forget
That he is man, ye ruffian hordes!"[18]

"Let bogus votes [19] and bogus laws [20]
   Stand as the will of God! Drive out [21]
   The villain cursed who talks about
   The 'Higher Law!' [22] Let him not spout [23]
His treason here! The righteous cause

"Of slavery is recognized
   By the first law of man and God;—
   Kansas we own, and on her sod
   Shall stand no man, unless he nod
To our great *Truth*, and be baptized

"And taken into fellowship
   With all the dear, beloved ones
   Who are not classed with Freedom's sons.
   Give to Northern men solid tons
Of iron hail! and then let slip

"The dogs of War! Let no church ope
   The door to him who cannot pray
   For Slavery's cause! [24] Let no man stay
   On Kansas soil, who casts a ray
Of heavenly light on sinking hope."

Brave Kansas! Now thy bitter hour
   Comes like a gale of piercing woe,—
   And where fair Freedom stands, the foe
   Unsheathes his sword. Her friends bend low
The neck beneath usurping power.

PARDEE BUTLER.

Strange craft appears upon the breast
  Of swift Missouri's stream,—a boat
  Of two logs made, bound fast to float,
  With Pardee Butler, who of note
Had made his name. Upon his crest

The letter "R" is stamped;—and flags
  Of divers kinds, with mottoes rare
  And quaint, lend to the ambient air
  Weird and vile visions of despair:—
But Hope cheers him while Justice lags. [25]

CHARLES W. DOW.

Now falls the innocent young Dow,
  Whose manly breast the fatal shot
  Received unarmed. No fiend, "come hot
  From hell," would his base honor blot,
With deed so base as this foul blow. [26]

WILLIAM PHILLIPS.

Brave Phillips, to the call of Truth,
  Protests against the fraud which made
  Proud Kansas fall within the shade
  Of Slavery's night, and he is laid
Beneath its heel with no relenting ruth.

Torn from his home, where tender ties
   Bind fast the heart,—borne to the den
   Of slimy Vice and Hate, and then
   Shorn of his hair, and bare as when
On earth he came, prostrate he lies,

A fresh victim to Slavery's cause.
   Game of the knights of *tar* and *rail!*
   Doomed to the auction block and sale!
   He passed a work of rare entail
According to the "bogus" laws.

This done, and sanctioned by a call
   Of Slavery's *"law and order"* men,
   A band of ruffians from their den,
   Into his bright home, where children
Clasp his knees, and tender cries fall

On his sad heart, and where dear wife
   Implores and prays, and where to save
   A life the law protects a slave
   As well as king, came this conclave
And there struck down a sacred life. [27]

THOMAS W. BARBER.

And Barber fell in rural shade,
   Where loving wife had taught to twine
   Around his door the blooming vine,
   Who shared his kiss in love divine
And his bright home an Eden made. [28]

How sad and cold the wintry day,
  When his soul passed within the vale
  Of death. The winds took up the wail
  Of grief, and bore it on the gale.
Then freemen gazed on his cold clay,

And called on Heaven, and raised the hand
  And swore to sow, and then to reap
  The seed which Freedom cast, nor sleep
  Till the avenging sword shall sweep
Her base-born foes from out the land.

ANDREW H. REEDER.

Then Reeder's life they seek.²⁹ The red
  Hand of Murder now waits to strike.
  His manly justice they dislike,
  And bowie-knife and deadly pike
Admonish him. Then sad he fled;

For he had learned to love this land
  Of blooming verdure and renown.
  'Neath shade of night, no name to own,
  Disguised, he stole away unknown,
Dreading the blow of Slavery's hand.

Then in his secret refuge waits
  For his escape, — what oaths he hears!
  What direful threats! what torture bears!
  What serves the honors that he wears?
All these would fall by Southern hates.

Now sees, within his recess dim,
  The dagger waiting for his life.
  How breaks his heart in secret strife,
  How yearns for home, where weeping wife
And waiting children pray for him!

THE INVASION.

Blow now the blast of direful War!
  Call in the hordes of "Southern Rights!"
  Come from Virginia's mountain heights!
  Come from the ocean, where delights
To float the flag with the "Lone Star." 30

And let Missouri now stand forth,
  A solid phalanx on the call
  Of sheriff! Let her bring her small
  Arms and weighty cannon, and all
Her chivalry, to crush the North. 31

LAWRENCE.

Why? Nestled in the lovely vale
  Where now the Kansas gently flows
  Serene, and where the lily grows,
  Like drooping Love beside the rose,
And where the powers of Peace prevail,

There Lawrence stands, a lovely queen
  Of May. Sweet Lawrence! Freedom's child!
  Cradled in love, and taught the mild
  And gentle ways of Truth, she smiled
In graceful beauty not unseen.

The love of man for man she taught;
 She taught that human rights are dear;
 She loved the home, and sought to cheer
 Sad hearts; and she erected here
A citadel for honest thought.

This was enough. With sullen look
 Great guns of war on Oread
 Frown down on her defenseless head.
 And now the baleful star has said:
"Her doom is writ in Fate's great book."[32]

Then came indictments and grave writs
 For treason, construction of, or high;
 Which had been found with legal eye,
 In ample form and quality,
And sanctioned by juristic wits.

So ordered by Lecompte, the great
 First Justice, Chief;—upon whose head
 Had clustered all the glory shed
 By Southern laws;—whose life was fed
On that rare meat, early and late,

Which doth enchant and chain the mind,—
 While Slavery had entwined around
 His heart,—and in whose smile he found
 That pure, sweet grace, which doth confound
Justice and those to her inclined.[33]

Three victims now for treason ³ ⁴ stand
   In proud sublimity,—each name
   Denotes its cause; its public fame;
   Its noble birth, and why it came
To do its work sublimely grand.

Free State Hotel— Kansas Free State—
   Herald of Freedom,—these the foes
   Of Slavery's cause;—here were the woes
   From "Bogus" laws denounced,—here blows
For Justice struck sublimely great.

"Blow up the fortress Freedom built!
   Let cannon roar! Tear down the wall!
   Cast out the press! The shattering fall
   Will silence speech! Set fire to all
Within, and crush the freeman's guilt!"—

These the hoarse shouts of Sheriff Jones.
   The savage work is done, and there
   The fiends of hell ride in the air;
   And frowning furies of despair
Shriek their shrill notes in dismal tones.

Carry the news, oh Crime! nor lag
   In thy hot haste, to herald forth
   The fall of Lawrence and the North!
   Now over all, in matchless worth
To Southern cause, the great red flag,

Whereon the lone star shines, there waves
  And flaunts insulting in the gale;—
  But Freedom, listening, heard the wail
  Of her three friends, and saw the trail
Of Treason passing o'er their graves. [35]

Lawrence, you yet shall drink the cup
  Of gall, and wear the weeds of woe;—
  You yet shall feel the savage blow
  And deadly shaft from Treason's bow,—
Yet go down and with Affliction sup. [36]

This past, the victor's crown shall wear.
  Lawrence, no more thy fate bewail!
  Sprung from the ashes, thee we hail,
  Immortal Phœnix of the vale!
And thy proud name and glory share.

Here shall our children joyous come,
  From Learning's ample fount to drink;—
  Perhaps from Euclid here to shrink,
  And with poetic Virgil, link
The Trojan race to that of Rome.

Or here in academic shade
  With Plato walk; or find tne school
  Where Athens' sage made wise the fool;
  Or trace beneath the tyrant's rule
Great states, and see their glory fade;

Or here, in some sequestered spot,
    The song and theme of poet praise;
    Or from the heights of Oread gaze
    On other worlds, and catch the rays
Of suns whose years bewilder thought.

FREEDOM'S CHAMPION.

Now the great Nestor of debate,
    The manly Sumner, stands with bold
    And godlike front, and there unrolled
    The scroll of Infamy, and told
How nations fall and how grow great,—

And waiting Senate listening heard.
    The Nation heard; and heard the foul
    And sodden South, who then with scowl
    Of visage dire sent forth a howl,
In answer to the heavenly word.

Kansas his theme,—of crime to tell,
    Which he flung down at Slavery's door.
    Then Slavery struck,—'t is writ in lore
    Of hell,—and down on Senate floor,
Beneath the blow, great Sumner fell. [37]

LIBERTY AND JOHN BROWN.

Then Liberty, who long had wept
    O'er crimes committed in her name,
    Took her sad flight from halls where Fame
    Had blazoned forth her deeds, and came
On sable wing of Night, where kept

Her sacred watch-fire burning bright
  On Kansas soil, the great John Brown.
  Him she found;—not in busy town,
  Or soft on easy couch lain down;
But on the grassy plain, where Night

With scent of flower and gentle dew
  Refreshed,—him sad and lowly bent
  In fervent prayer, and turbulent
  Unrest she found;—then flashing sent
O'er him her radiant light, and threw

Her armor down, and thus began:
  "Great friend of man and liberty,
  My name and cause shall honored be
  In this broad land from sea to sea;
Soon shall Slavery's course be run.

"But ere that time, a mighty hand,
  Well worthy of the Titan race,
  Must here be raised, and in the face
  Of Treason break the lance, and chase
Its furies howling from the land.

"Here in the shade of sacred Night,
  With all her stars and heavenly train
  Of worshipers who brightly reign
  On high to note, thy soul I chain
To my great cause, and give thee sight

"And holy light to see divine.
   On thee now falls the blessed ray
   Which gilds my shield, and naught shall stay
   My onward march, until the day
I love shall here in glory shine.

"Thee have I called, like John of old,
   Who the dear Savior's course forerun,—
   And thee baptize my holy son,
   With fire, in name of Holy One.
Now here within my hand I hold

"What the great John of Patmos said
   Should be in time outpoured on earth,—
   Vials of wrath;—their deadly worth
   Is needed now,—for fierce from birth
The serpent old holds high his head.

"Into this vial now I put the tears,
   Which loving wives and children shed
   In Kansas, o'er their murdered dead.
   Here is a lock of hair from head
Of Sumner, with fresh blood it bears;—

"Here is the blood of murdered Dow,
   Barber, Brown, [38] Jones, [39] and Stewart brave;
   Five sons of mine now in their grave,—
   This pang their passing spirits gave
And cried in woe: 'Make Treason bow!'

The Song of Kansas.

"Here is the anguish of their hearts
  Which through my drooping spirit runs;—
  Here are the groans these dying sons
  Have left, and prayers for darling ones,
And kiss while ebbing life departs;—

"Here the torn flesh and bloody scars,
  And damning insult Phillips stood;—
  From Butler's craft a piece of wood;—
  Here is a drop of virgin blood
Ravished by fiends beneath my stars;—

"The ashes here of Lawrence,—there
  The type of press, the drunken glee,—
  The dust from trail of Treason see;—
  Here is the bullet shot at me,
And here the slimy serpent's glare.

"These 'Bogus' votes you see were cast
  By ruffian hordes, and these their rags;—
  Here the ruffian words on flags;—
  Here the hoarse laugh while Justice lags,
And here the 'Bogus Laws' at last.

"All these into this vial go!
  Now soak, and shake, and let distill.
  Behold another one I fill!
  Here from the sword of Bunker Hill
Drops the base blood of foreign foe;—

"Here is the sigh which Warren gave,
  As his sweet spirit passed on high;—
  Here the keen glance of Putnam's eye;—
  Here Franklin's thought; and here the cry
Of Henry: 'Freedom or the grave!'

"Here the patriot pen of Paine,
  And here the deeds of Washington;—
  Here are his battles lost and won;
  And here the dust of every son
Of mine who in that cause was slain;—

"Here the swift shaft which Jackson sent
  Full at the front of Treason;— here
  The hot words which Tallmadge, dear
  And grand to every freeman's ear,
Hurled back at Cobb, and fatal went. 40

"This is enough. This vial keep;
  For you will need the lighter drink
  When Death shall take you home; nor sink
  Beneath the awful thought; nor think
The draught not good; for your last sleep

"Shall come and pass in awful form;
  And you shall heave the broken sigh,
  And grandly on the scaffold die,—
  Then with the patriots you shall lie,
Unmindful of the passing storm.

"But here, this darker drink now quaff!"
This then she handed him, and Brown
Arose and said: "The thorny crown
I wear, nor do I seek renown,—
The stormy path I tread, thy staff

"Supports me now;"—and then he drank.
This now infused all fear forsook,
And all his vital spirits shook.
Then opened he the Holy Book,
And said: "Great Author, Thee I thank

"For counsels in my hour of need:
'An eye for eye, and tooth for tooth,'
This is no fond, no gentle ruth,
No smooth, gilt-edged or varnished truth—
Within this book I find my creed;"[1]

"Its counsels wise shall guide my feet.
'Tis written here in holy word:
'Christ came not peace to bring, but sword,—
To Him I bow, as my great Lord.
His truth is ample and complete."

This said, the goddess took her flight,
And back on sable wing she sped,
With flashing halo round her head,—
By fair Columbia's hand was led
Through all the glittering train of Night.

Great soul inspired! whet now thy sword,—
  Not in revenge, but to protect
  The land, where Freedom may erect
  Her home; where safely her elect
May come and live in sweet accord.

This is the land where first began
  The holy work in Virtue's cause,—
  Where men demanded righteous laws
  And justice unto all,—here was
The sword once more unsheathed for man.

Not like the sword of cherubim,
  Who stood of old at Eden's gate,
  To guard the path against those great
  First trespassers on God's estate
In earth, as sung in holy hymn;—

That was a flaming sword of fire,
  Drawn by ghostly hand, and could
  Not stand the test of steel, nor should
  We deem it more than that which would
In rain or weeping dew expire;—

But here on holy Kansas soil,
  Stout hearts, and kind and true, were made
  To seek the virtue of a blade,
  Keen as old Damascus, which stayed
The march of ravenous fiends of spoil.

It was a blade two-edged and strong,
  And sharp and true, as that which rung
  In Gideon's hand, by poet sung,—
  It was the blade which Justice hung
O'er sinful heads, and deeds of wrong.⁴²

A blow in retribution struck
  Now falls:—for those five sons who died
  In Freedom's cause, five from the side
  Of Slavery now shall pass the tide:—
No hand of Pity tries to pluck

Them from his grasp,—no kindly call
  Of Mercy can his blade elude,—
  Savage it fell, and sharp and rude,
  As Samuel into pieces hewed
King Agag, with the sword of Saul.

Sweet month of May! thy tender hand
  Now spreads the verdure of the year,—
  The rose and vine twine am'rous near
  The door; the song of bird we hear,
And midst thy blissful beauties stand.

At such a time, in sylvan shade,
  The sword of Justice fell. The stroke
  Crashed through the serpent's scales, --it broke
  The deadly coil, and curling smoke
And flaming fire bespoke the blade.

Now Freedom's sons stand forth once more,
   Encouraged to protect their homes,—
   And in her weeds the widow comes
   To urge, and tears of little ones
Brave fathers kiss away, implore,

For sturdy hand and manly heart,
   To wage the battle of the North,—
   And it was done. And then came forth
   The power for deeds of solid worth,
Which forced the monster to depart.

In writhing agony he went,[43]
   With brutal Murder in his path,—
   No mercy now, no pity hath!
   And coiling fierce in fire and wrath,
Seems Hell on dire destruction bent.

Aloft the bloody scalp he waves,[44]
   The dripping blood rests on his brow,—
   Kills the poor cripple at his plow,[45]
   And swears to make all freemen bow,
Or send them bleeding to their graves.

But hark! It is brave Walker's voice
   As he commands, and stern report
   Of Freedom's guns as they on fort
   Of Titus belch their fiery sport.
A shout: 't is "Freemen, now rejoice!"

The type from Freedom's press are cast
For Freedom's guns, and back they fling
The leaden speech on fiery wing.
Lecompton fell! No one may sing
Her praise,—damned by a name at last. [46]

COL. JOHN W. GEARY.

When manly Geary said: "I know
No North, no South, no East, no West,
Nor aught but that which serveth best
For Kansas; this is my behest,
That right and gentle peace may grow;

"That war may stop, blood cease to flow;
That we as men must stand or fall
Beneath one flag which waves for all:—
Nor ask of me that I recall
The fierce, foul harvester of woe."

Scarce did he dream that the foul blow
Of deadly knife for him should wait,—
That the red hand and direful hate
Of Slavery would carve out his fate,
And scourge and fill his life with woe. [47]

And why? No flag does Slavery know,
But that which waves for Southern cause.
The starry flag rebukes her laws!
Nor any land wins her applause,
Where seeds of Treason will not grow.

Teach Dis to smile! Foul Treason wed
   To Justice! Paint beauty for the blind!
   Give demons heavenly words and kind!
   The hundred-headed Hydra bind!
This is what Geary tried, and fled.

LINN.

And now we see the bloody hand
   And torch pass over beauteous Linn,— [48]
   For there had come to dwell within
   This garden spot brave men, whose sin
It only was to bravely stand

By Freedom's cause. With fond intent
   To build their homes, here by the side
   Of peaceful stream, or prairie wide,
   Or where the oak in forest pride
Outstretched his arms, they pitched their tent.

And here where Little Sugar winds,
   And gently flows in graceful sweep,
   'Neath rugged hills that, high and steep,
   In sylvan shade and grandeur sleep,
His sacred home the patriot finds.

Nestled beneath these ancient hills,
   Whose beauties challenge foreign lands,
   In landscape made by heavenly hands,
   The friend of man, MOUND CITY stands,—
Her history with rapture thrills.

Hannah H. im. pinx. OSAWANDA.

Home of Montgomery! who here
The battles of fair Freedom fought, —
Sacred the soil, and dearly bought
By blood of her brave men, who thought
Their liberty as life is dear.

OSAWANDA.

'T was on the Little Osage, just below
The point at which the river, winding slow,
Touches the belt of rocky timber hills
Which stretching far away to westward fills
Out the landscape of prairie grove and glade.
This touched with morning light and passing shade
Made pictures fairer than a painter's dream,
Through which the ready rays of Nature gleam.
Here happy June with sweetly-scented breeze
Had decked the earth in green, and blooming trees
Lit up the scene, and set with vernal flame
The flow'ry picture in a leafy frame.
Here Genius bold, aspiring to be great,
Drops the tired brush, and Nature strikes in hate
The hand of him who tries to imitate.
To such a spot as this in Kansas came
Young Rubin: Northern blood, and sturdy frame
Inured to toil, a will for any fate.
Thus stood a living factor of a State
To be, — which prophesied by such as him
Should come, — not in the ages dim,

But soon,— and panoplied in Freedom's dower
Of righteousness, and girt about with power.
First, here into this valley fair he came,—
The first to mark the bound'ries of his claim,—
First to select the spot and cabin build,
With soul elate, of fairy fancies filled.
Then in his many wakeful dreams by day,
Which ran like some unpastured colt at play,
While to his axe the nodding trees would bow,
Or while a-field and plodding at the plow,
He caught the vision of a blissful home,-
A home where young and happy wife should
    come,—
Where barns were full and plenty cheered the board
And where his title deed should own him lord.
'T was thus he mused and thus he pictured all,
And hung the picture on his cabin wall.
Such men are in demand and win their way
To wealth and power, to love and song, and play
With Fate as reckless as a truant boy
O'erleaps the rules of school, or laughs for joy.
Nor are they sought in vain. The neighbor goes
To such in faith, and breathes his painful woes
Or pleasures soft into the willing ear,
And finds a friend who ne'er disdains to hear.
There the glad soul may list to pleasure's lay
And joyous wile the happy hours away:—
Or aching heart may plaint its doleful psalm

Of life, and find the ready unctuous balm
Unstinted poured on wounds by one who shares
His weary ways, and mournful, cumbrous cares:—
Or here, when hearts awake the conscious flame
Of mated love, responsive to the heavenly name,
May feel the fervor and the power divine
Of *Home*, where all the cares and bliss of life com-
  bine.

'T was June, as I have said before,
 And somehow Rubin's thoughts would turn
 To love,—the thought would Rubin spurn.
  Untaught of Love, how could he learn
Without some angel at his door

To light this candle of the soul?
 But there would come to him, untaught,
 The vision of some hallow'd thought;
 Some fairy form by fancy caught,
Which stayed beyond the will's control.

Then would he heave the heavy sigh,
 As in that vision he could trace
 The rounded form, the living grace,
 The luster of a shining face,
The flowing hair and flashing eye.

Thus with some book of modern lore,
    He musing sat, beneath a high
    Old oak, whose shadow, creeping by,
    Seemed to the stranger drawing nigh
To point a welcome to his door.

The stupid leaves he fumbled o'er,
    But dallied with Love's dream of old,—
    His mind the pages could not hold;
    And when he raised his eyes, behold!
She stood before his cabin door.

Dumb and transfixed he sat, while he
    Beheld his fairest thought fulfilled.
    Oh! for the ready brush of skilled
    Hogarth, to catch the scene that thrilled
His trembling spirit's phantasy.

Glossy and black as raven's wing,
    Was her bounteous flowing hair.
    Down o'er her neck and shoulders fair,
    It softly fell, that these might share
The woman's wealth the Graces bring.

Here fell on his enraptured sight
    The full-orbed glory of her eyes;
    Whose modest lids in soft surprise
    Half hid the blue which mocked the skies.
Her clustering teeth, faultless and white,

And half-confined by ruby lips,
　Laughed within their pearly bed.
　Beauty flies round the radiant head,
　And, like the bee by passion led,
Dies in the nectar that she sips.

Her hand was small, her waist was trim,
　The hat was jaunty; and bestud
　With leaves and grasses of the wood;—
　And a wild flower with opening bud
Was lurking just beneath the rim.

Gracefully from her dapple gray,
　Which saddleless she rode, she dropped
　Upon her slippered feet, and stopped
　Before the door half-open propped,
To greet the owner with "Good day."

But ere she had espied him, he
　Came up; and in a bashful way
　Thus said: "How do you do to-day?
　A little dandy dapple gray
You ride! What can your errand be?"

Startled, and coyly, she replied:
　"My father sent me here to know,
　If you would come to-day, and go
　With him, to warn a family or so
To leave the creek,—they are deep-dyed

"Abolitionists, so 't is said;—
   And at a meeting held to-day,
   It was ruled that they cannot stay,—
   But before *I* would go away,
If them, I would fight till I was dead."

"What is your name, if I may ask,"
   Said Rubin with a twinkle in
   His eye,—"Come here and sit within
   This shade, and tell me what the sin
So great, that I must do this task?"

So saying, he took the bridle rein
   Of Gray, and led the blushing maid
   To a rustic seat, within the shade
   Of that old oak, which he had made
The campus of his new domain.

She bashful said: "My name is Ruth,—
   But still I have another name,
   To which I answer just the same;
   And I like it better,—for it came,
If the Osages tell the truth,

"Just like a snowflake from the sky.
   Now pardon, how it is so dear
   To me: My father came out here
   Some years ago to hunt the deer,
When only ten years old was I.

"Mother and babies too, all went
    With hunters then,—father was out,—
    I left alone to run about
    The camp, when came an Indian scout,
And stole me from my father's tent.

"Soon was I tied upon a horse,—
    Terrible and tiresome was the ride,—
    Well I recall the prayers denied;
    And how I plead, and moaned and cried,
To waken pity or remorse.

"But all in vain. Would Heaven forsake?
    No. Sleep to me her blessing gave,
    And in the morning a young brave,
    Kneeling o'er me, said: 'Now I save
OSAWANDA,—pretty snowflake.'

"How he saved his little Snowflake,
    Need not here be told,—he became
    My guardian friend;—no other fame
    He sought,—and I love the name
Of Osawanda for his sake.

"Five years o'er sandy plains to roam,
    We swept the desert side by side,—
    This was his choicest steed, his pride,—
    This gave to me,—this did I ride
In his long search to bring me home."

Transfixed, intent to hear, and charmed,
   Was Rubin in his rustic seat;
   While Osawanda, bright and sweet
   As a May morn, told in a neat
And airy way how she, unharmed,

Was brought home to her father's door.
   While she thus poured into his ear
   Her lay, a mocking-bird, with clear
   Unbroken notes, whose mate was near,
Poured forth, as upward he did soar

From the topmost branch of that tall
   Oak, his heavenly, amorous song:—
   Then in mid air — as if his long
   Drawn strain had storm'd his passion strong,
And thrilled by his own notes, in all

Their flood of melody — would fall
   From air to tree, and falling die
   Of his own song in ecstasy;—
   But they were deaf to the wild cry
Of bird, and his melodious call.

That mighty tyrant of the heart,
   Eros, had come. The captive chains
   Are there, with all their ruby stains;
   And all the arms of him who reigns
By the tragic splendors of his dart.

The Song of Kansas. 51

Now, through his spirit wildly roll,
   In fierce delight, the forces that
   Are felt in love and war; which at
   Her touch he felt, as there he sat,
In the focus of her burning soul.

Then Rubin quickly to reply,
   Patting the face of Dapple Gray
   To him softly said: "And I must say
   I love you, for your rider gay
Hath charmed me with her dark blue eye."

Then he to Osawanda said:
"Fair one, should I join in this raid
   Against the homesteads which are made
   By other honest men? This shade
Is not more dear to my poor head

"Than theirs to them. No. I will not!
   Tell your father that in this world
   There's room,—that vengeance shall be hurled
   On him, when o'er his head is furled
The flag of freedom,—and a blot

"Shall stain the coward soul of him
   Who will not stand by human rights;—
   That honor crowns his life who fights
   For that in which *Fair Play* delights,
And all the world his praises sing.

"Sweet Snowflake! let your mission be,
   Like thy pure name in mercy given,
   A white-winged messenger from heaven,—
   Let not homes from them be riven
Whose hearts now beat for Liberty.

"Let your mission be peace, not strife.
   To this just end be quick to dare;
   And to protect this *Snowflake* fair,
   With all that in me lies, I swear
By the charmed story of your life."

While thus he spoke, he gently took
   Unconsciously her hand,— the fair
   One conscious, and his zeal to share
   Thought him most grand, and charmed him
      there
By the mute eloquence of her look.

But now the lengthened shadows came
   Which told that Nature's day was done,—
   And as the summer hours are run,
   And harvests ripen in the sun,
So in the rays of Love's full flame,

In those eventful summer hours,
   Which softly ran unconscious by,
   Hath ripened into ecstasy
   Two hearts, which now shall pant and sigh
For stolen interviews, and shady bowers.

The Song of Kansas.

She took the reins: "Down! Kansas, down!"
 She said, and Dapple, bending low,
 Received her with a graceful bow.
 Away she swept, but on her brow
There sat the shadow of a frown.

"A new world!" Rubin cried aloud,
 As on she sped among the trees;—
"A world which one not only sees,
 But seeing loves, like the soft breeze
In balmy June, with floating cloud."

Osawanda was called plain Ruth
 At home, for there no other name
 Would answer, even though it came
 Full of old romance, or in flame
Of love, or deeds of tender sooth.

And then the ready way wherein
 Young Rubin always called her by
 Her Indian name, seemed now to lie
 Close to her heart,—and her blue eye
Sparkled as she thought of him.

At home, she met the cold and stern
 Rebuff,—that roughness which denies
 The tender, soft amenities,
 Which speak in smiles, and laughing eyes,
And tones which loving hearts discern.

And then she mused while going home,
    How Rubin said that she was fair,—
    And how he praised her flowing hair.
    Oh! what a change to mortal pair,
In one sweet hour of love will come!

But now, the Fates fly round the hour!
    'T was late when she arrived at home,—
    Long had they looked for her to come;
    And in their weary waiting, some-
How overlooked the latent power,

Which lay within the melting heart
    Of this young girl's fresh womanhood;
    Which, when evoked, is not withstood,
    When she is in the tender mood,
By all the outward forms of art;—

And they dreamed not that Love, with his
    Seductive arts, might counterfoil
    Their schemes, by digging in sweet toil,
    Within that garden, whose virgin soil
Productive is of mysteries.

The father sternly thus began
    "Ruth, you're late! Did you notify
    That scamp about what's in our eye?
    These fellows must all leave or die."
"Yes," said Ruth, and away she ran,

With Dapple to the shed; for she
    Was then unable to control
    The bursting tumults of her soul.
    O Time!—give time! and back will roll
The dashing waves of this high sea.

Alone with Dapple, she began
    To try her voice,—pet names by rote
    Would call, and stroked his glossy coat,
    But found her heart still in her throat.
Heart of stone in breast of Indian,

Struck by the anguish that she felt,
    Would then have broken by the stroke.
    But Dapple fed,—her fresh song broke
    Forth upon the air, and awoke
The hills, whose liquid strains would melt

In soft, returning notes, and fall
    An echoing cadence from afar
    On the charmed ear. Never at war
    Was heart so sad; never did mar
With song so sad, the soul's sweet call.

Clear did the woodland echoes bring
    The charming sound of song she sung,
    In sonnant, soft Cigiha tongue,—
    And loud the melting words were rung,
Unknown by all who heard her sing.

SONG.

Wananda the great gave me a bird,—
  A bird from the forest at even,—
    Sweetly he slept my bosom adorning,
    And awoke with a song in the morning.
Two years did I keep him, but the third,
  He flew to Wananda, the keeper of heaven.

And I pray to Wananda the great,
  To send back the bird that was given,
    For now sad in my soul there is ringing.
    The sweet broken song that he was singing;
Ere he flew far away to the gate,
  That opes to Wananda, the keeper of heaven.

Now Life's Great Trail I follow all day;
  And sadly I slumber at even;
    For I lie all alone and forsaken,
    Since my bird from my bosom was taken;
Sadly I sing and fervently pray,
  Return him, Wananda, the keeper of heaven.

A meeting there that night was held,
  And called for purposes of state,—
    And to consider crimes of late,—
    And settle and decide the fate
Of sundry new settlers, and weld

The ties of a confederate
  Brotherhood; defensive in form
  Of word and call; but in the storm
  Of backwoods eloquence, and warm
Declaim, it took the form of hate,

Toward every person, high or low,
  Who was allied to Freedom's cause.
  Then one began: "Who burnt our laws?"⁴⁹
  And while they listened at the pause,
An ancient owl cried: "Who! who! h—oo!"

This was enough:—for there outside
  As sure as ears can hear, and tongue
  Can mock, must be the foe. Then young
  And old, for valor yet unsung,
Rushed out to hunt him far and wide.

No enemy they found, for he
  Had flown; but there in spectral white
  Stood Osawanda, in the light
  Of moon full orbed,—a fairy sprite,
Listening for fate in secrecy.

Then to the council she was led,
  A willing witness to the truth.
  "Come," said one, "tell the meeting, Ruth,
  About this Rubin; is the youth
Sound on the goose? Is he corn fed?"⁵⁰

The tumults of her soul had passed,—
   The fears of an impending fate,
   Which brooded in her soul of late,
   Gave way to full-fledged scorn and hate,—
Then came the thunderbolt at last.

An old toad-haunted cabin was
   The place in which the council met;—
   And there with flickering rays beset,
   A fancy work of art, did fret
Its rustic walls—*The Bogus Laws,*

Whereon a tallow dip did stand
   On end, there struggling to enlighten
   This pit of darkness, and to brighten
   This book, which long had stood to frighten,
Until its conflagration grand.

And this lone candle burning dim
   Scarce threw a shadow on the floor,—
   But came the Moon with beam she bore,
   As if this darkness to explore,
Was prompted by some heavenly whim.

The latch string to the clapboard door
   Was pulled inside. On blocks of wood
   Sedately sat the court;—their good
   Old coon-skin caps, but tailless, stood
Beside them on the puncheon floor.

The Song of Kansas.

And in the corner, pale as ghost,
   Such as our aged grandams might
   Have seen against the rayless night,
   Stood our *Snowflake*, with eyes so bright,
The moonbeam in their light was lost:—

Who thus began: "On errand sent,
   With questions heavy, and of great
   Pith to this young and coming State,
   And such that I could scarce relate,
To find young Rubin forth I went.

"This very day I met him, and
   The message gave,—with courtesy
   Received, I thought I could descry
   A trembling twinkle in his eye,
As there my soul he did command.

"We then discoursed of naught which this
   League cares to know:—enough to say,
   It was of birds and garlands gay,
   Until the shadows of the day
Slow-length'ning vanished with my bliss.

"But this I caught and will relate,—
   Proudly erect he stood and tall,
   And said: 'I build a home though small,
   For wife to find,—nor ill befall
My love, nor freedom of the State.'"

Then a hoarse murmur of dissent, —
A growl, as of some wild despair,
Like a chafed tiger in his lair,
Came forth upon the silent air,
From men upon destruction bent.

"Ho! this young rascal, now," said one,
"Will set at naught our government!
For what business be we here sent?
We will take care of this young gent!
Come, boy! hand up to me my gun!"

Then she replied: "Questions of state
Are not for me. Little I know
Of book, or law, or league, and so
I never give them thought; and slow
I bring my mind to catch debate, —

"But one thing above all I know, —
That woman's work goes with her love, —
And where her heart leads, like the dove
From Noah's ark sent forth to prove
The land, there her swift wing will go.

"Guard your Rubins, and the houses that
They build, where loves may safely nest;
Then the young State will proudly rest
Upon the Nation's love and breast,
Like the famed ark on Ararat."

The Song of Kansas.

Quickly now was this night's work done
  In that debate, and with that sure,
  Savage purpose, which doth allure
  The mad mob, and a vote secure,
As if it were the voice of one.

The night was set,—the silent hour
  Was named for work,—naught should conflict,
  Save now some heavenly interdict,
  As sure as should that hour be ticked,
Upon the clock of Time's great tower.

They all retire, and Ruth withdrew
  Unto her sad and restless bed,—
  And there she mused, spinning her thread
  Of fancies one by one, till dead
Rubin's face broke the thread in two;

Then dropped her hand upon the head
  Of her huge hound, which long had been
  Her friend; going and coming in
  Captive life, like some faithful kin,
And always slept beside her bed.

He, conscious of some trouble there,
  Within his young queen's throbbing breast,
  Moaning, licked her hand, and in quest
  Of truth arose, disturbed of rest,
And put his paw upon her hair.

She kissed his hand, and then arose,
   And looked upon the moon-lit world
   Without. Silent as the infurled
   Whisper of a secret wish curled
Close to her heart, she reached her clothes.

In that soft, still hour of midnight,
   Silent she dressed; and with such fear
   Of bold intent, and to her heart so near,
   She dared not let the angels hear
Her thought, lest them it might affright.

Now past the open door, — no thought
   Or look behind, but soft she sped,
   With footfalls of a fairy's tread,
   For Dapple to the open shed, —
Dapple who knew her will untaught.

Easy and slow, and sure she rode,
   Till past the house and hovel by
   The brook, then loosed the rein, — a sigh
   Of wished relief, — a half-pent cry,
Which until now had been a load

Upon her heart, she uttered low.
   And now she flies, a passing sprite,
   Like some weird wonder of the night,
   Along the plain, in the pale light
Of the mellow moonbeam's glow.

The Song of Kansas.

Halting a little at the ford,
   To let her "*Kansas*" feel his way;
   The rippling waters seemed to say:
"Good girl! good girl!" in gurgling play,
"Go on! go on! you serve the Lord."

The cabin reached; she knocked, and spoke
   In softest tone: "Is Rubin here?"
   "Yes," he replied; "who do I hear?"
And then awoke; but it was clear
To him a dream his slumbers broke.

A moment's hush, — she then replied:
   "Dress! be quick! and beneath the oak
   We'll briefly talk." The spell was broke,
As there with trembling voice she spoke, —
And Terror saw the dream denied.

'T was but a moment ere the tree
   He reached, and she at once began:
   "Your life is sought, and so I ran
To tell and aid you all I can.
Death can't outrun my love for thee."

He seized her hand, — spell-bound and dumb
   He stood, — and as he looked to eyes
   That shone like moving orbs, which rise
And set at sea, and whose light dies
At morn, presaging day to come,

He could do nought but stand and look;
    And yet more firmly, kindly press
    Her hand. At length, a lip caress
    Thereof was taken *sans* duress;
Nor did she chide for what he took.

This broke the spell, and then she told,
    At his request, at length and all
    Of that which at the council's call
    Was done, or should or might befall.
Then said: "This thought I uttered bold:

"'But one thing above all I know:
    That woman's work goes with her love,
    And where her heart leads, like the dove
    From Noah's ark sent forth to prove
The land, there her swift wing will go.'"

Then his pure passion broke control,—
    And thus in flood of ecstasy,
    As there he saw within her eye
    And daring face his destiny,
Poured forth the torrent of his soul:

"Would that my heart were that loved land,
    And thou the dove in search of rest;
    Then would I be forever blest,
    When she should find it, there to nest,
And share the bounties of my hand."

The Song of Kansas.

Then she replied: "But foes have said
   That you shall have no land to till;
   Nor nest for bird, nor barn to fill;
   Nor bounties to bestow at will,
Though small, with which the bird is fed."

Then he: "But foes may go and come;
   The brave alone Heaven's bounties share;
   The coward never won the fair;
   Sweethearts are won by *do* and *dare;*
With this my life, my love, my home.

"Without courage, how would it be
   Here on thy sacred mission pure
   To save my life?   Could you endure
   The savage cry of Slander, sure
With pack to bay thy purity?

"Courage is queenly grace to woman given,—
   The godlike flame in which all slander dies,—
The path whose gentle slope leads up to heaven,—
   The gemmed Orient of her hopeful skies.

"For neither will the world, nor her warm heart's
   Desire, trust to the fragile arm of Fear;—
And as the hunted doe at bay now starts
   To find retreat, knowing that death is near,
—5

"Will fall an easy prey to all the pack;
    So sure should Innocence, sweet as the flower
Opening its soft petals to the sun, lack
    Strength, she'll fall by Slander's rude touch
        and power:

"But the stout heart, however frail the form
    Within whose white-robed vestal zone it be,
Will, like Egypt's pyramids, outlast the storm,
    And save the sacred name of Purity."

Then she: "Your soul is brave and free.
    I'll be your bird, for you have caught
    Me on the wing; and you have taught
    Me love:— Now fight for life! I've bought
Its fee,— then trust in Heaven and me.

"To-morrow night they come,— be on
    Your guard,— reason and overcome
    Their rage with fair persuasion; some
    Are taught by truth, while some are dumb.
Sweetheart, good night." And she was gone.

Thus, in the solemn stillness hushed
    By dreamy after-thought of Night,
    Two Kansan hearts, intent on right,
    Guided by Love's pure flame and light,
Into each other's life have rushed.

The Song of Kansas.

The morrow dawned upon the mob.
　　Little did Osawanda dream
　　That she could counterfoil their scheme,
　　With aught that she might say or seem
To them,—for hell was in the job.

But every move she did discern;
　　And every word and thought expressed,
　　She noted; and her rage repressed;
　　And betimes her huge hound caressed,
And played a careless unconcern.

But as the evening shades appeared,
　　Four men, each a desperate fiend
　　In human flesh, came up and leaned
　　Upon the fence, and so demeaned
Themselves, nor hell nor death they feared.

Aloud they called for "Old Kaintuck;"—
　　And now they drink, and yell, and stare
　　And roar, and swear as devils swear;
　　And call it pure and red and rare;
And as they drink they say: "Here's luck."

Then boasted o'er that drunken bowl,
　　That one "white-livered" Free-State man
　　Should die that night; and then began
　　To load their guns. Now guess, who can,
The terror that convulsed a soul!

Ruth quickly turned, and put her hand
  Upon her heart; then fell beside
  Her faithful hound; and he espied
  Her dreadful agony, and tried
To talk; but she could understand,

And fainted not,—but quickly as
  An inspiration from above,
  Sent down by some angelic love,
  She had resolved. No soft kid glove
For pets; but lead the virtue has.

Now for a ride to outrun Death,
  Whose stealthy footsteps quickly fall
  Upon her ear. Hope, life, love, all
  May go; for nothing can recall
His stroke, nor melt his frozen breath.

Time! O for the full power to stop
  His clock, and cheat grim-visaged Fate,
  Who stands like chiseled law to wait,
  Cold, sullen and disconsolate,
To keep the time, and slip the drop.

Dapple she rides, whose mettle oft
  In other days and scenes was tried,—
  Joy of her heart, her pet, her pride,—
  On darkness gaze they far and wide,—
The plain before, the stars aloft.

The Song of Kansas.

One star she knows of all the host,
  Which has to millions been a star
  To guide to fame, to love and war,—
  That polar light which shines afar,
To point the way, or find the lost.

Out from the woods, and northward start,
  Like hunted deer,—and on they rush,
  Heedless of mound, or brake, or bush;
  For Dapple knows in whispering hush
Her fears, and feels her throbbing heart.

And as he glides she softly talks:—
  "Now gently, Dapple,—gently—slow—
  Not too fast at start—far to go,
  And fearful is the way,—you know
We must not fail—*fail!* That word locks

"My lips! *To fail!* O Heaven! let not
  The faintest whisper of that word
  Among the starry host be heard!
  But let my speed be like the bird,
Whose flight fulfills her swiftest thought!

"Kansas, my pride! you never saw
  Me fail! and you shall have the rein.
  You saved me once upon the plain
  From wolves; and once from being slain
By bison on the Ninnescah.

"But then *my* life is all there was
 At stake. Now my life rushes toward
 A life that resteth on the sword,—
 The faithful servant of its lord;—
Then take the rein, and speed his cause!"

Far past the Elk, and to the brow
 Of Little Sugar's circling hills,
 Down whose rough sides dire Terror fills
 The passing soul,—yet dauntless wills,
And on they plunge, till safely now

Upon the bosom of the broad
 Valley spread out in green below.
 Then to the northward on they go,
 Till Little Sugar, rippling slow,
Arrests their speed. This crossed, unawed

Into the forest, west by a single path
 They go, and eager winding, thread
 Their way, until their rapid tread
 Is heard by one whom ruffians dread,
Against the vengeance of his wrath.

'T is Colonel James Montgomery's fort.
 "Halt! who comes there?" is uttered loud
 Within. "A friend,"—responded proud
 Our Ruth, with ready wit endowed—
"And I'm in search of brave support."

The Song of Kansas.

"A brave support!" then answered he;
"I'll do my part if just the cause;
But I obey no "Bogus" laws,—
I have cast them into the jaws
Of hell. What can your errand be?"

"To quickly save a noble soul
From the ruffian jaws of hell,"
Responded she. "But now, please tell
How am I to know but some fell
Plot of knave is laid to enroll

"My name with the unnumbered dead,
And you the sweet-faced angel fraud?"
A moment dumb, then— "*O my God!*"
Broke from a heavenly soul outlawed
Of earth, and heart subdued with dread.

It was a wail of such wild woe,
In plaint of doleful anguish caught,
That the stern warrior doubted not
That she was all she told and thought,
And said: "Ah, well! my maid, I go."

But now she said: "Last fall I shot
A buck with you on yonder hill;
And in the trial of our skill
With gun, both shot, but you did kill,
And won the deer, but took him not."

"You are the Osawanda, then;
　　The fair, black-haired, and blue-eyed maid,—
　　The captive child!" the chieftain said.
"I am," said Ruth.　"You have my aid,"
Said he, "against a thousand men."

Soon on their way were rushing fast,
　　Down where the Little Sugar flows,
　　With wild bird's song and scent of rose,—
　　On through woods where the maple grows,—
And on till frowning hill is past.

There checked their speed for moment's breath.
　　Then asked of Ruth: "What now to thee
　　Is this young man? some kin to be
　　Perhaps." "Worlds! worlds!" said she,
　　　"to me,—
And for his life I race with Death."

Then she cried: "On! my Kansas, on!"
　　Then he: "And save! my Beecher, save!"[51]
　　Who knows by what kind power the brave
　　May live, or foul may find his grave?
Both come to earth, and then are gone.

Now we leave, dashing white with foam
　　Their steeds,—and turn unto the four
　　Fiends we left two hours before.
　　These drunken, and athirst for gore,
Have found their way to Rubin's home.

The Song of Kansas.

And in those two dread mortal hours,
  The insult and the pain he bore
  Within the threshold of his door
Cannot be told. Why fate deplore?
Or ask the why of hidden powers?

Enough for mortal man to know:
  Him stripped and tied, his flesh they gashed
  With knives and sharpened sticks; they lashed
  His back with whips; and swore and gnashed
Their teeth, and mocked him in his woe.

To the kind voice of Reason dumb,
  The prowling beast some mercy has;
  But to these fiends pale Pity was
  A painted plaything for a devil's jaws,—
They drowned and drank it in their rum.

But Rubin said: "Give me a chance,—
  Four to one is not fair, when tied.
  Untie; I ask not aught beside."
  This was refused, and then they cried:
"Come, boy! give us a song and dance."

Then at last one put his hard hand
  On Rubin's heart, and cried: "Gods, men,
  How it thumps against his ribs!" Then
  He put his ear close, and again
He cried: "Gush! gush! it lacks the sand."

And then he drew his knife and said:
  "Now, boys, this knife I whet to-day
  For blood. Its point is sharp to slay;
  It's time for it to drink,—give way!"
And high it gleamed above his head.

But the base hand, quiv'ring on high,
  Staid,—and to the floor the knife's fall
  Went, harmless; for a navy ball
  Had pierced his heart. 'T was the close call,
Unerring, of Montgomery.

Then and there three ruffians died.
  The fourth was saved, but notice took
  Of what Montgomery said: "Now look,
  You fiend, and note it in your book:
Henceforth, your horde must hunt and hide."

These were Montgomery's terms, and long
  The subtle foe obeyed. The maid,
  With Rubin saved, stood undismayed,
  Angelic in that midnight shade,
And there entwined, with passion strong,

Her hero in the arms of love.
  The claim they held, and long thereat
  They lived, and mighty men begat
  Who stand for blissful home; for that
Holds Freedom's ark; and ark the dove.

The Song of Kansas.

Montgomery, thy manly shade
  Now rests in peace. The sacred grove
  Now decorates thy grave in love;
  And weeping waters gurgling move
Close to thy feet where thou art laid.

Thy watchful eye and daring hand
  Guarded the way for Liberty,—
  Here at the gates of Linn we see
  Thy stalwart blade and standard high,
'As thou a sentinel didst stand!

Sweet be thy rest! and while the years
  Roll round, thy name in memory green
  Shall live, and here each year be seen.
  Thy comrades come, and o'er thee lean,
And drop the tribute of their tears.

JOHN BROWN.

Sad Linn! Dark plots and direful things
  In secret hatched, and compacts made
  In the vile den or sickly shade,
  And writ with point of Slavery's blade,
In bloody book which Treason brings.

In this black book appears the name
  And sentence of each Freedom's son,—
  Boldly in blood the letters run,
  In the fierce hand of Hamilton.
Now stands to his infernal fame

The record of that bloody book:
    Eleven blasts from hell are blown,—
    Eleven teeth of dragon sown,—
    Eleven sons like grass cut down;
And Hydra of his feast partook.

Then came John Brown close on his path,
    And boldly passing to his den,
    Him struck an awful blow, and when
    The shackles broke and fell from men
He writhed and roared in demon's wrath.

Eleven slaves are now set free,—
    A kindly stroke for those who fell,—
    A just and righteous parallel,— [52]
    Their freedom won, and strange to tell
Kansas has gained her liberty.

Not on far Afric's burning sand,
    When age on age has come and gone,
    And people searching in the throng
    Which passing centuries prolong,
Ask for some hero proud and grand,

The theme for master sculptor's hand,
    Whose ancient glory and renown
    The waiting multitude shall crown,
    Will there remote appear John Brown;-
But will be found in every land

The Song of Kansas.

His glory heralded by seers,—
  In marble cut; by poet sung;
  And his rude image shall be hung
Round the charmed neck, and every tongue
Shall praise him as the saint of years.

And here, in Kansas, we shall raise
  The statue to undying fame.
  With sculptured art, we shall proclaim
  The fond memorial of his name,
Which thus shall stand and speak his praise.

The man—the sword,—the Hydra slain,—
  The hand outstretched to greet
  The needy one,—the face replete
  With love,—and, underneath his feet,
The broken links of Slavery's chain.

Bright star of Kansas! now thy place
  Is fixed:—a brilliant central gem,
  In Columbia's diadem;
  Which, like the star of Bethlehem,
Points out a savior of the race.

O Slavery! dire, enraged;—if you
  Are doomed, what serves to now rebel?
  What serves the powers that wait on hell?
  You sent the shaft when Sumpter fell,
Which on recoil shall pierce you through.

THE CIVIL WAR.

Behold two little clouds which 'rose,
    And in the sky o'er Kansas stand;
    They seem no larger than the hand,
    But soon they grow, and o'er the land
Spread out a shroud in dark repose.

These clouds are fierce and filled with wrath,—
    One at the southward, clad in gray,
    Is shimmering in the lightning's play;
    And lowly muttering makes his way
Northward, and coiling in his path:—

The one at northward clad in blue,
    Like some dark monarch on his throne,
    And grumbling in his baritone,
    Through rifts of clouds which he has blown
About his head, takes notice due.

Now these huge monarchs of the air
    Approach, and rise in awful form;
    And as their fury seems to warm,
    They clutch,—then bursts the awful storm.
Great giants from ethereal lair,

In fierce embrace, now twist and coil
    In brawny arms which never tire:—
    Now crash the thunders in their ire,—
    They fling their livid wrath in fire,
And make the whirling cyclone boil.

The Song of Kansas.

Then blow their all-subduing breath
  To earth, and round and round they leap —
  And, eastward bound, black ruin heap
  On wild despair, — and waltzing, sweep
In weird and wicked dance of death.

Thus say: The solid South conspired
  To rule the North. Sad was the day
  They clutched, — and wicked was the way
  To peace; but when it came, the gray
Had in the Northern grasp expired.

And say: That Kansas, in the war
  To save Columbia's home, in time
  And men stands first, —[53] that she did climb
  Vast heights to fame, nor any crime
Nor halt her battle-flag doth mar.

IV.

KANSAS IN THE REIGN OF PEACE.

PEACE.

Our Iliad of woes is past,
   And gentle Peace, with healing wing,
   Now comes with all her arts to bring
   Repose; and softer notes I sing,
While Hope looks up from Ruin's blast.

And from this wreck of civil strife
   And war, where Treason dying lies,
   Behold two manly forms arise!
   No cold, disdainful look replies
To that sad wail of human life;

But with kind hand that stoops to save;
   And face lit with benignant smile,
   That doth grim-visaged War beguile;
   The flag that Treason would defile,
They spread o'er its eternal grave.

With modest look and humble pride,
   Thus Grant and Lincoln stand;— and there
   Between, two other forms more fair:—
   Columbia with her flag in air;
The *private soldier* close beside,

In rich, immortal blue. At rest
He half reclines,—and you can trace
A sad smile lingering on his face;
While the fond goddess wreaths in grace
His head, there pillowed on her breast.

THE STATE.

Great kings may die and empires fall,—
 Races of men come on the stage,
 And pass away in sickly age,—
 Ancient and dim is History's page
And hard to read; the print's too small;

But what is great, and what endures,
 Is built by all. Those truths and deeds,
 Though small, collected like the seeds
 Of earth, and saved for future needs,
Are then not mine alone, nor yours,

But do belong to all. The State
 On these is built in grandeur bold,
 And stands in time by cycles told,
 While workmen's names lie in the mold
Of age forgot, or small or great:—

As polyp rude, beneath the waves
 Builds her coral home, and lays
 The deep foundations where we raise
 The fabric of the State; the praise
We cast upon forgotten graves.

Thus you will find where'er you roam
  Within some quiet spot select,
  The soldier's grave; nor name detect;
  No fame he sought, but to protect
His flag, his country, and his home.

The flag sustained and country blessed,
  Was greater than to reach a throne,—
  His life was but his country's own,—
  He sleeps upon her breast unknown,—
In quiet glory let him rest!

THE HOME.

No spot so dear on earth as home.
  We build the home; this builds the State.
  This loyal makes the Nation great,—
  And all from love. No hand of Fate
Builds, or pulls down a nation's dome.

No happy footsteps from the home
  E'er trod the path which Treason takes.
  No hand from happy fireside shakes
  The murderer's blade, nor it forsakes,
To Cæsar kill, or rule great Rome.

Kansas, in this thy glories rise,—
  In this thy strength. Thy people here
  Their plain and humble structures rear,—
  They plow and plant at home, nor fear
That there an execution lies.

What though their earthly lot is hard!
What though their humble house be sod!
They bend no knee to tyrant's nod;
There they may live and worship God,
And love shall never be debarred.

Husbands and wives, and little ones,
Are kings and queens on Kansas soil,—
Their empire rests secure from broil,—
And here in peaceful life they toil,
And raise for Liberty her sons.

'T is here that lisping children come,
Now sad to tell some little care;
Or pleased the parent's kiss to share,
With little hands and flowing hair,
Braid links of love around the home.

'T is sweet to know that here the State
Protects the home,—that she has thrown
Around the hearth and wife her own
Strong arm,—that this no kingly crown
Could do, no more on grandeur wait.

And when the fee vests in the wife,
It is a badge of love, not fraud;—
And when for home, let courts applaud!
'T is hers, where every household god
May rest secure, and bless her life.

As well destroy the tree which shades
   Her door; the nest of bird whose song
   Enchants the grove; as there to wrong
   Her love, and all her griefs prolong,
Which once was done by legal raids.

Take not her household gods away!
   Her lot is hard enough at best;
   At home, let each fond object rest
   Beneath its wing! Here is the nest
Of love! For this we fight and pray.

Nor shall the curse of drink, *strong drink*,
   Whose pain is as the adder's sting,
   Sure, quick and deadly, ever bring
   To Kansas home its guilt, and fling
The household gods on ruin's brink.

This has made Kansas great, — to this
   She owes her growth, her power and wealth;
   Her brawny arm and sturdy health;
   She gains by prowess, not by stealth,
And home brings all her victories.

In legislative halls by hand
   Of artist touched, where fretted dome
   And classic pillars charm, do come
   The great defenders of the home,
And round its fires a bulwark stand.

The Song of Kansas.

No wonder told in fairy tale,
  In web and woof of fancy wrought,
  Can equal this,—no vision caught
From fairy-land enchants the thought
Like this, in which our souls regale!

THE EARLY PIONEER.

Brave men here came to stand or fall
  For Liberty. The silver ray
  Of Hope shone bright upon their way;—
  With faith unshaken, here to stay,
No flesh pots could their steps recall.

Heroes they came! to combat here
  The fates and furies of vast Hell.
  Unto a desert land to dwell
  They came; nor drouth, nor flood, could quell
Their earnest rage for Freedom dear.

False signs to scare did fill the breeze—
  At crossings of old Indian trails,
  The traveler reads: "Every crop fails;"—
  "It never rains;"—"Sometimes it hails;"—
"Timothy won't grow, nor trees."

At these the sturdy pioneer
  Leveled his axe; and with a stroke
  Cut down the lies; and then he broke
  The sod with plow and steers, and woke
The earth to grow his harvests here.

But ere the harvest came, what toil
   Here taxed his early hours and late!
   What cares and fears on him did wait!
   Ere he the fickle hand of Fate
Could guide, and fix it in the soil.

THE PRAIRIE FIRE.

'T is said Prometheus filched the fire
   From heaven to minister unto man;
   But in its use the godly plan
   Became a scourge, and fire outran
The fierce revenge of heavenly ire.

Thus, when the white autumnal frost
   Had touched the world to tints of brown;
   And blue-joint grass, in tasseled down,
   Waved its long plumes; and for a crown
The Year, these silken tresses tossed,

I've seen upon the Kansas plain
   In early years the fiends of fire
   Let loose,—who in their hot desire
   To curse the world did melt in ire,
And break the elemental chain.

Out from the portals of the south
   They came. No blast from Borean caves,
   Beneath the cool, refreshing waves
   Of northern sea,—but fiercely raves
The dread *South Wind*, with whom goes *Drouth:*

The Song of Kansas.

Weird sisters of the sandy plain,
  Who scourge the land with fiery thong,
  And, moaning as they pass along,
  They chant their sad sirocco song,
And chase away the gentle rain.

The blue October haze that slept
  Upon the grassy fields had passed
  Away,—and then a somber cast
  Came on, with swift-winged storm, and fast
These frowning furies onward swept.

Then on the land they blew their breath,
  And fanned it with their fiery wings;—
  No weeping rain, no siren sings,
  But from the surging flame there springs
The black and horrid form of Death.

Far as the eye can reach the world
  Ablaze,—a vast and billowy sea
  Of fire,—and there aloft in glee
  These furies danced in revelry,—
Their heads in fiery tresses curled —

And smoke black as the Stygean blast,
  And tongues of fire shot forth, and bore
  Aloft the food of flame it tore
  From earth,—and on with thundering roar
And hiss and crackling noise they passed,—

Their way black as the path of hell.
    The wolf sought refuge in his den,
    And safe the wing of prairie-hen;
    But the poor deer to reach the fen,
With fleetest footsteps, fainting fell.

Thus was the land left black and drear,—
    Thus was the food cut off from herd,—
    And home burnt up of man and bird,—
    And husky voice of dearth was heard,
For fire had harvested the year.

The faint-heart croaked: a thought did swerve:
    His wife had people in the East,—
    Egypt had flesh pots for a feast,—
    He went. Thus was the land released
Of him, and saved by men of nerve.

THE HEROES.

Of heroes Kansas is the child!
    When Freedom's banner was unfurl'd,
    Then on her doubtful soil were hurl'd
    Gods of the intellectual world,
Who stood by her till Fortune smiled.

Brim full of health, to hardy fare
    Inured, with purpose pure and high,
    They did their work without a sigh,
    As if made, and then sustained, by
The unseen energies of air.

The Song of Kansas.

No more the hot sirocco blows —
  The farmer stopped it with his plow;
No drouth disturbs the drowsy cow —
  The planted grove shades her, and now
The desert blossoms like the rose.

COMMERCE.

Each day her glory like the sun
  In splendor comes; the ready hand
  In field and forge now waves the wand
  With magic power; and through the land
The thundering wheels of commerce run.

Mighty black monarchs of the plain, —
  Great giants with Briarean arms;
  Whose throats belch forth volcanic charms, —
  Steel-shod they tread with wise alarms,
And pull the lengthened, cumbrous train.

These mighty engines of the brain
  Have brought fair Fortune here to stay, —
  Have decked the State in bright array,
  With golden grain; and roundelay
Has ushered in the golden reign.

THE FLAG.

Great State! thy work shall never lag,
  For here Columbia's royal mace,
  Advancing, leads her stalwart race;
  While overhead thy star in place,
Shines brilliant in our country's flag.

No flag so great on earth as this!
  Go where you will; in every place
  It honored is;—no hand so base,
  As mar its fair and starry face,
Which angels seeing stoop to kiss.

Let it in splendor from on high
  Glance on the world its starry beams!
  It now in faith and glory streams,—
  It has fulfilled the patriot's dreams,
And flaunts in heaven's fair face no lie.

How beats in love the soldier's heart,
  As he beholds its folds unfurled;
  For it the battles of a world
  He fought, when Treason's lance was hurled;
And broke beneath his feet the dart.

Proudly erect the bearer stands,
  As o'er his head the colors wave;
  For this his sword is drawn to save;
  For this he dares to find his grave,
While it floats heavenward from his hands.

Let it go forth to every land!
  Let it in starry splendor wave,
  O'er every honored patriot's grave!
  Let it in every ocean lave!
And be unfurled by every hand!

HISTORY'S WISDOM.

Down the long aisles of ancient time
  We tread, and view upon our way
  The old historic milestones day
  By day;—some here half-broken lay,
Sad relics of a distant clime,—

Some there but half erect recline,
  Bending beneath the weight of age,—
  Perhaps the deeds of saint or sage
  Record,—perhaps the warrior's rage,
And on his cruelties refine:—

Whilst here again some shaft is found
  With letters dim, which doth allure
  The eye,—it fell by that obscure,
  Sad touch, which makes oblivion sure,
And lies half buried in the ground:

Or here now comes upon our sight
  A pillar lettered o'er with fame
  Of one, whose long-forgotten name
  Does like some mummied thought exclaim:
Behold the meteor's passing flight!

Name of wise man or nation great,
  On tablet writ, or on the face
  Of obelisk; their fame we trace,—
  The same sure stroke which doth erase
The one, so marks the other's fate.

Throw back the veil! let in the light
   Of enthean fire on peoples great!
   On city, kingdom, or on state,
   O'erthrown by man, or God or Fate,—
It lights them to eternal night.

Of such wise lessons Kansas conned;
   And learned to shun the rock and shoal
   Of that dark sea, where ceaseless roll
   The waves that lift or whelm the soul-
Filled ship:—her hope is Virtue's bond.

Nor lift the dark, mysterious veil
   Which shrouds the realms of future day:
   Haunt not, without some wise delay,
   Those precincts lit with holy ray,
That glints upon the hopeful sail.

Count not, dear friend, the grand array
   Of millions as they proudly swell
   The time-worn rolls, and safely dwell
   On plain, or in the flow'ry dell,
With peace,—and happy in their day:—

Enough for us to know; their homes,
   Blooming like flowers on Kansas soil,—
   Warmed by the fires of honest toil,
   And lit with lamp of Wisdom's oil,
Are safer than the gilded domes.

The Song of Kansas.

THE SUNFLOWER.

Land of warm hearts, and true and bold;
Of yellow corn and golden wheat;
Where rosy morn, in radiance sweet,
Casts the Orient at her feet;
And happy colors run to gold.

Blooming land where the sunflower reigns
In grace and splendor unconcealed!
While sister flowers their homage yield,
And crown her goddess of the field,—
The bright Aurora of the plains.

Along the paths of commerce old,
She stands a sentinel and queen;
Streaking the landscape's lovely sheen,
With tints of yellow in the green;
And blooms in beauty and in gold.

THE PATRIOT'S LOVE.

Proud Kansas! known on land and sea;
Happy the man on foreign strand
Who hails from thee! In any land
On earth, a Kansan let him stand,
This name shall be his passport free.

Kansas! I love thy sacred name,
As o'er my memory sweeps the past;—
From thy dark, deep trouble thou hast
Now come, to glorious peace, and vast
Domain, and everlasting fame.

The Song of Kansas.

I dearly love thy stately frame;—
    That grand physique of prairies wide,
    Which, like some undulating tide
    Of mighty sea, billows in pride
Thy lovely form, and breathes thy name.

I love thy soul,—that spark divine
    Which struck from the Almighty mind
    Illumines earth, with manners kind,
    And motives pure, and laws refined,
And Justice sure, and love benign.

The home of freemen thou shalt be,
    Where patriot footsteps love to stray,
    And to thy soil their homage pay,—
    Where Virtue with her heavenly ray
Doth shine in sweetest purity.

And when Time comes to end my days,—
    Chant in my ear some old refrain
    Of patriot song;—the parting pain
    Will cease;—then say: "In humble strain
He sang for Kansas her sweet praise."

Miscellaneous Poems.

Miscellaneous Poems.

THE PRAYER UPON THE WALL.

TO MRS. ELIZABETH H. ROSS, OF CHICAGO, ILL., THIS POEM
IS DEDICATED. JULY 25, 1888.

I. UNDER THE LIGHTS.

As I SAT within my home,
Turning o'er some ancient tome,
Mousing at the musty-lore,
There beside me on the floor
 Sat my wife, with a
Many-colored zephyr ball,
 And she stitched away,
On a motto for the wall.

One by one the letters spelt
A prayer, asking Him who dwelt
In the high cerulean dome,
Every day to bless our home.
 "God Bless our Home," she
There with threads of zephyr ball,
 Like skilled Arachne,
Wrought this motto for the wall.
—7

Humming to herself the while,
"Spicy breath", and "Ceylon's isle"—
Scent of flowers and song of birds
Blended with the holy words.
    Thus her hand unsought,
All my senses did enthrall,—
    Hand that deftly wrought,
Holy words upon the wall.

Then I heard her softly say,
In her quiet, tuneful way:
"Have I inwrought God's design,
With this needle here of mine
    Into every strand;
And will now a blessing fall
    From the heavenly Hand,
For this motto on the wall?"

II. WITHIN THE SHADOWS.

Dimmed the eyes that brightly shone!
Hushed the voice of sweetest tone!
Gone the hand that deftly wrought,
Letters for a blessing sought!
    On the threshold lie
My griefs; and I there recall
    Her sweet prayer, by
The silent motto on the wall.

The Prayer upon the Wall.

Trees and flowers and grassy lawn,
Greet the birds at break of dawn;
And within the somber shade,
Still the nest of love is made;
    But my bird is flown,
Far beyond her mate's recall,
    And faded flowers strown,
Mock the motto on the wall.

Birds no more for me will sing,
Flowers bloom not in the spring,
Home shall be no home to me,
Blessings shall I never see;
    Sad I sing my lays,
For the charming life of all
    Haunts me as I gaze
On her prayer upon the wall.

Still I sit within my home,
Turning o'er the ancient tome;
Searching for the hidden lore,
That, may stricken hearts restore.
    Nor healing heavenly dew,
Nor Gilead's balm let fall,
    Can bless like one who
Placed her prayer upon the wall.

III. THE BROKEN HARP.

Touch not the harp! its chords are broken,
    Its sweetest tones are dead;
Like holy words of love unspoken,
    It is a prayer unsaid.

Or strike the chords of sinking sadness!
    Responsive to my soul;
For I am tossed on waves of madness,
    And wild the billows roll.

Like harp within my home forsaken,
    My life is all unstrung;
Or like the voice no harp can waken,
    It is a song unsung.

The soul that now is touched with sorrow,
    Is like a flower unblown;
Its hopes are rainbows of to-morrow,
    Which span the great unknown.

Yet, while my heart like harp is broken,
    I sometimes think withal,
That prayer was by an angel spoken,
    Which hangs upon the wall.

DAWN.

AND Night, who treads the vaulted dome, threw o'er
   My soul the shadow of her lifted hand,
   Veiling my vision from her starry land;
And closed from my fond hope that golden shore,
   Whose spangled pathways I should walk no more.
Then did the heavens recede, and all the grand
   Infinities of worlds that there expand,
And left me groping at her temple door.
Then I flung down my faith in man and God;
   But when I turned to drink from Lethe's cup,
Prophetic DAWN, whose feet are sandal-shod
   With heavenly light, forbade my soul to sup,—
She chased the shadows with her roseate rod,
   And led the Morn to lift my spirit up.

THE TEAR.

She weeping dropped a tear, and when it fell
   A poet caught the little pearly sphere
   And questioned it; and his enraptured ear
Caught up the things which it began to tell.
He heard the tone of solemn sounding knell
   O'er a departed Hope; the cry of Fear;
   The wail of Anguish; and soft sighings dear
Which make the lover's lonely bosom swell.
And there he saw ensphered a mother's heart,
   Bleeding for her lost child; and open grave,—
And Love amid the trophies of his dart,
   With every throb of passion that it gave.
All heights of joy, and depths of woe, were here
Encompassed in the ocean of a tear.

LIFE.

A POET wandered on some shore of time,
And there in numbers wrote in mimic hand
The story of a life upon the sand;
But soon the tide washed out the poet's rhyme.
A fair sweet flower within its proper clime,
   Alone, unseen, touched by some magic wand,
   Drooped its fresh face and wept upon the land.
Poet and flower alike is life sublime.
But whence, O Life! come these fair things, the
   flower
That blooms, the bard who sings, the sea, the sky,
The scenes of love with their enraptured hour,
   When everything of earth is born to die?
There is no Œdipus with godlike power,
   To guess the riddle of Life's mystery.

THE LAST ROLL.

During the closing hours of the Senate, in 1883, it had been suggested that the next roll call would be the last of the expiring session. The thought occurred to the author that a poem would be proper at this juncture. A hastily written one was submitted privately to Senator H. C. Sluss, who pronounced it worthy of the occasion, and moved that the Assistant Secretary be heard immediately after the call of the last roll. After it was read Senator A. R. Greene offered the following resolution, which was unanimously adopted: "*Resolved*, That the poem, with the roll of the Senate attached, be spread upon the journal, and that five hundred copies be printed for the use of the Senate."

The gavel came down, and a look of sadness
    Came over the President's face;
And the noisy rattle of mirth and gladness
    Was hushed, while each one in his place,
Felt around his heart creeping a sorrow past his control,
As the President said: "Secretary, call the last roll!"

Here are now gathered from out this fair land,
    A senate of forty strong men:
Farmer, doctor, lawyer, merchant, now stand
    With work done — a work that no pen
Can undo, until Time writes on his old battle-scarred scroll,
The work of a world all done, and *his* call of the last roll.

The Last Roll.

Now is the time when all differences cease,
    All faiths and religions are one;
And each high Senator gives a release
    Of all past claims under the sun
That he had on his brother, in pledge of word, deed or dole,
And shakes hands freely all round at the call of the last roll.

Each hobby goes out, lean, lank, and unsaddled;
    Each man is the peer of his brother;
All issues now end, e'en those that were straddled,
    While souls now embrace one another; —
And the fierce face of politics the old flag doth enroll,
And heart beats to heart kindly, at the call of the last roll.

No more to all meet on this rounded ball,
    No more in this Senate all stand
To be counted, — you have heard the last "call";
    And now comes the time to disband, —
And I think many hot tears are welling up in the soul,
As you now hear, and respond to the call of the last roll.

But I ask: Down in the dim future years,
   On the shore of some fair Eden-land,
May you not all meet,— a senate of seers,
   And clasp the affectionate hand?
Ah! in that dim depth of the future, that fate of the soul,
Who knows but I may call to you all the old Senate roll?

ROLL OF THE SENATE.

ALLEN, H. M.
ANDERSON, T.
BENSON, A. W.
BLUE, R. W.
BOLING, T. G. V.
BRADBURY, L.
BREYFOGLE, L. W.
BRIGGS, L. M.
BRODERICK, CASE.
BROWN, N. B.
BUCHAN, W. J.
CASE, G. H.
CLARK, A. B.
COGSWELL, A. P.

COLLINS, IRA F.
CRANE, B. M.
EVEREST, A. S.
FINCH, L. E.
FUNSTON, E. H.
GLASSE, W. B.
GREENE, A. R.
HACKNEY, W. P.
HOGG, B. F.
HUTCHINSON, PERRY.
JOHNTZ, JOHN.
JONES, M. T.
KELLEY, HARRISON.

LONG, J. C.
MC LOUTH, A.
METSKER, D. C.
MOTZ, SIMON.
PATCHIN, A. L.
RECTOR, J. W.
RIDDLE, A. P.
SEXTON, J. Z.
SLUSS, H. C.
THACKER, S. O.
WARE, E. F.
WILKIE, NEIL.
WILLIAMS, B. M.

UNIVERSITY OF MICHIGAN.

DEPARTMENT OF LITERATURE, SCIENCE AND THE ARTS.

A poem delivered June 27, 1888, before the class of 1858, at the reunion after thirty years.

THE CLASS.

FRANK ASKEW.	R. M. JOHNSON.	BROWSE J. PRENTIS.
LUTHER BECKWITH.	DANIEL KLOSZ.	OSCAR F. PRICE.
HENRY A. BUCK.	A. J. LOOMIS.	J. E. PRUTZMAN.
H. B. BURGESS.	HENRY F. LYSTER.	W. E. QUINBY.
E. B. CHANDLER.	GEO. A. MARK.	A. RICHARD.
GEO. M. CHESTER.	LEWIS MC LOUTH.	S. E. SMITH.
GEO. M. DANFORTH.	O. H. MC OMBER.	J. T. SNODDY.
H. J. DENNIS.	C. R. MILLER.	A. K. SPENCE.
J. Q. A. FRITCHEY.	JOEL MOODY.	JAMES W. STARK.
T. G. GAVIN.	ROBT. S. MOORE.	O. P. STEARNS.
JOHN GRAVES.	JUDD M. MOTT.	GEO. P. SWEET.
WESLEY A. GREEN.	C. W. MYKRANTS.	B. U. THOMPSON.
HORACE HALBERT.	A. NEFF.	GEO. W. WALL.
L. E. HOLDEN.	L. M. O'BRIEN.	D. B. WEBSTER.
JOHN HORNER.	J. W. PAINE	F. R. WILL'AMS.
M. E. N. HOWELL.	C. S. PATTERSON.	W. S. WOODRUFF.
H. A. HUMPHREY.		

THRENODY.

I.

THE Years; daughters of Time, have laugh'd
  And wept in circling 'round,
Since we were students here, and trod
  This classic college ground.
Came they in garb of flow'ry May,
  Or whitening wintry snow;
With wreath of bay or daffodil;
  Came they to reap or sow;
The flow'ret here to cast that cheers,
  The ashes there of woe;

Their fleeting forms went swiftly by,
    And thirty in their turn,
Have dropped the off'ring of their hands
    Within the golden urn.

II.

Recollections holy! how like
    A troop of angel forms
Arise, bringing the olden times;
    And all our being warms.
To see the fond, fair pictures that
    They hold to Memory's eye;
Turning the thought to dear old scenes,
    As they go glinting by.
At this, convulsed, we happy laugh,
    At that, we heave the sigh;
While now some fairy stands in view,
    And Memory loves to dwell
With sacred form that haunts the soul,
    And charms with magic spell.

III.

Backward through years; and now we ask
    As there transported stand
Upon the boundary of some
    Far-off enchanted land:

What hallowed sound is that which comes
  Upon the waves sublime,
Now gently falling on the ear
  Like some old mystic rhyme,
And sets our spirits all a-dancing
  To its rhythmic chime?
Breathe not the word to earthly forms;
  To heaven its virtues tell;
While Thirty Years ring out: the *tone*
  Of dear old college bell.

IV.

How sad the thought, as now we go,
  Boys again, arm in arm
Down through the college grounds and halls,
  Striving the ancient charm
To find; striving alas! in vain.
  The old cannot be found;
Nor ancient seat where once we sat;
  Nor open college ground;
Nor bell that rang us out and in
  With its melodious sound.
Little the use of coming back
  To search for ancient joys,
For all we find of what was here,
  When we were college boys.

V.

Gone is the dear old chancellor: boys
    Were we of Tappan's pride:
The *me* and *not me* of his lore,
    These too are laid aside.
Wisdom, he told us, is to grow;
    And little were the odds
When Reason's' great informing law,
    Which working in the clods
Of flesh, transports the souls of men,
    And lifts them unto gods:
To grow in beauty and in grace,
    Not cumbering the ground;
But stalworth plants of earth, reaching
    To heaven, with honor crowned.

VI.

Wise were the lessons that he taught,
    And with benignant care;
And quick to grow within our souls,
    The seeds he scattered there.
Wide and generous was his thought,
    Clasping the human race:
Deep was his love; and we could read,
    As beaming on his face,
Came the true story of his heart,
    That there we had a place

August he stands like holy sage,
    In majesty of soul,
Pointing to Truth; and bids our names
    In her great book enroll.

VII.

High hopes and will for any fate
    Inspire, as now we stand
On great commencement day and take
    The parchment from his hand.
How on the mental vision crowd
    The freighted scenes, which hold
Their places in the chambers
    Of the soul, and gild the old
With their fantastic hues, and deck
    The dark with threads of gold!
Now o'er his grave in foreign land,
    We bow in sorrow there;
Nor comes the blessing from his hand,
    Nor from his lips the prayer.

VIII.

How hath it fared with us since then,
    When with elastic tread,
We passed the threshold of these halls
    With halo 'round our head?

Wide is the world, and many a voice
    Invites us to the prize;
Fame with his clarion notes, and War
    Invites where patriot dies:
And fairy Fancies call, and high
    The stars of Glory rise.
Into the depths of life's great sea
    We plunge, and on its waves
We ride o'er sunken hopes, and see
    Their wintry, watery graves.

IX.

The halos 'round our youthful heads
    Soon vanish into air;
And all the clustering laurels fall
    That we had gathered there.
Then on the dusty road of life,
    Some went to earn a name;
And long they sat beneath, and conned
    The finger-board of Fame.
The path they took to right or left,
    To them was all the same;
The one who reached, and he who failed,
    Soon found what Tappan said:
Is hunger of the soul, and wailed
    At last for heavenly bread.

X.

The star of Glory too doth pass
    Before our waiting eyes,
Like falling meteor seen awhile,
    Then on the vision dies:
And all the Fancies of our youth
    Now wreathe the brows of Fact;
Who stubborn stood upon the road,
    And bid us dare to act:
While he the coward struck with blade,
    And him who virtue lacked.
He bid us reap in life's great field,
    And harvest home the sheaves;
For Autumn comes at last, to strew
    Our paths with withered leaves.

XI.

And War hath called, and many went
    The Nation's flag to save.
In honor all we stand, but some
    Adorn the patriot's grave.
They answered to the bugle's call
    And to their country's prayer.
Now at their graves we sadly meet
    And lay the garland there,
Wreathed by a classmate's hands in love,
    And with a soldier's care.

Brave children they, who went to die
    Upon their country's breast,
And sleeping there, in glory lie
    Within her arms at rest.

XII.

Dear class of Fifty-Eight, clasp hands,
    And with the warm, firm grip
Of friendship, let the old wine of
    Thirty years touch the lip.
Here are we met, mellowed with age
    And ripened to the core;
Again to part; perchance to meet
    When life's brief work is o'er,
With those who passed its boundaries
    To some Arcadian shore;
Perhaps within that realm unknown
    To find life's better part;
If not, Hope dying shall condone
    This token of the heart.

OLD CAPTAIN SUMPTER.

The following poem was recited at the camp fire on the evening before the unveiling of the soldiers' monument at Mound City, October 24, 1889. Governor L. U. Humphrey, to whom the poem is dedicated, received the original manuscript. Captain Sumpter died suddenly, while telling his little grandson about the war. He was a member of the military order of the Loyal Legion.

"Grandpa," said little Sam, as he came in
From play, "were you a soldier of the war?
And did you stick to Uncle Sam and win?
And did you get that great, long, ugly scar
Upon your face by standing to your colors true,
While you did march, and fight, and wear the soldier's blue?"

"Why do you ask?" said Sumpter old and gray;
"Come to my side, my boy, and tell me why
Such thoughts as these do thus disturb your play?"
And as he spoke there stood within his eye
A trembling tear, which sparkling shone like morning dew;
"Why do you ask about the war, and those who wore the blue?"

"Because," said little Sam, "we boys play war;
We drum, and march and fight with wooden guns;
And then our captain wears a shining star,
And says: 'Be brave! the man is killed who runs!

Stand to your colors like a Union volunteer!'
And when the enemy is hit and falls we cheer!

"And then you know, on Decoration days,
   The pretty girls do come with flowers to strew
The graves of soldiers dead, and rich bouquets
   They tie with ribbons — red and white and blue,
The colors of this button here in your lapel,—
And place them on the grassy mounds of those
      who fell."

The tear then dropped, and fell on Sammy's brow;
   But the soldier's eyes were fixed upon the sky,
And wore a dreamy look, as if somehow
   To scenes of other years — to days gone by —
His thought had turned entranced, and lingering
      far away,
On things grown old perhaps, but not to him
      grown gray.

"Yes, my lad," he then began, "hear me now:
   When Sumpter fell I saw my flag go down;
I saw the patriot blood on Ellsworth's brow,
   Which now immortal wreaths of glory crown;
And as he tore the traitor's flag I saw him fall,—
Then as a voice from heaven I heard my country
      call.

"Your father was a little lad like you,
    Not in his teens; and sister running round
And prattling every word of love she knew:—
    At such a time, at home, I heard the sound
Of fife and drum, that mustering rolled from sea
        to sea,
And patriotic words of Abe that called for me.

"Then to defend the starry flag I swore—
The flag for which I saw my country rise—
Sadly I lingered at my cabin door,
    And lingering looked through tears to tearful
        eyes;
How could I then from wife and little ones depart,
When beating drum was drowned by the beating
        of my heart!

"But Heaven gives strength to man in times like
        these—
    They said I went for fear the boys would lag—
But one acts sometimes better than he sees;
    And what is home without the patriot's flag?
It is a place in which tempestuous tumults roll;
Or palace built by man without a human soul.

"For this I left to weeds the planted corn,
    The plow forsaken in the field to rust;·
And with a prayer to God for lambs new shorn,
    Into His hands committed I the trust;

And oft a thought would turn to dear ones left
   behind,
And oft the thought: If killed, will the Nation
   then be kind?

"On Shiloh's bloody field, in Vicksburg's vale,
   And in the clouds on Lookout's dizzy crest,
We met our country's foes, and told the tale
   Of battles won by soldiers of the West;
Then from Atlanta marched for honors yet to be,
Until our banners kissed the waters of the sea.

"Stayed not the march, but up toward Lee we
   turned,
   A thundering, fighting phalanx, 'hot from hell,'
But Grant took him for whom our banners burned,
   And Treason there at Appomattox fell.
Sammy, you are well up in school, you know the
   rest,
But I was a Union volunteer and a soldier of the
   West.

"Then came the grand review at Washington,
   When Peace lit on the flag all battle torn;—
And when I think on all the battles lost and won,
   The comrades dear, and lives and loves outworn,
The famous names that live upon the Nation's
   scroll,
The flag is worth them all, the mistress of my soul.

"This button is an emblem of the flag;
  The flag an emblem of a patriot's love;
And while my weary hours through life I drag,
  I'll wear it like a sacred charm above
My heart." He ceased; his voice had to a whisper died,
While the fond hand, unclasped, had dropped from Sammy's side.

His cheek fell soft upon the youthful brow,
  Like age supported by the youthful limb;
"Please tell me more," said Sammy, "please," but now
  The ear heard not the tender call to him.
Life's floating flag was furled o'er drooping head;
His soul had joined the "Loyal Legion" of the dead.

THE GUEST AT HOME.

There is a guest true hearted who comes,
    Be the day ever so dark or so fair,
    And spreads o'er my face her curtain of hair;
While strains of old songs she soothingly hums.

Then on my bosom she tenderly lies,
    And presses her love-prayer warm to my lip;
    While softly her dark lashes sweepingly dip
Into the deep rivers flooding my eyes.

No voice do I hear, no form do I see;
    No warm hand to press, nor kisses to share;
    No footfall to greet, and vacant her chair;
But still in my home she cometh to me.

The world may say I'm alone and forsaken;
    But little it dreams of the angel who cheers,
    And brings to me, laden with perfume of years,
Both lily and rose, old loves to awaken.

THE SAWMILL OF THE GODS.

This poem was recited by the author at a banquet given by the alumni of the University of Michigan, May 23, 1890, at the Coates House, Kansas City.

"The mills of the gods grind slow."

THE sawmill of the gods saws slowly the tree;—
No matter how hard or how soft it may be,
Nor the kind, whether oak or basswood or pine,
The sawdust comes out of it almighty fine.

And noiseless it runs as the hourglass of Time;
And sharply it cuts, and its work is sublime;
For high on Olympus this sawmill doth stand,
And ever it runs by an almighty hand.

On the timber of mortals it saweth away;
And ever it saws by night and by day;
And it faithfully saws up all kinds of wood,—
The infernal bad and almighty good.

Trees that storms and lightning have ruined and rift;
Rotten of heart; and slimy deadwood and drift;
Old haunts of the vermin, where the woodpecker
    lurks,
Are sawed in this mill where the Almighty works.

And the buzz-saw therein shines bright as the suns,—
Forged by old Vulcan,— and like lightning it runs,
With this notice above it lettered in chert:
"The man who here monkeys gets mightily hurt."

And there an inspector stands silent and sad,
To divide all that's sawed, the good from the bad;
For says an old saw: "In the mills of the gods,
Between good and bad there's an almighty odds."

And the one who divides, divideth it well;—
The sap, shake, and slabs he slides into hell;
But the sound he saves for the house of the god,
Who shaketh the earth with his almighty nod.

And in the divide of the sawed it is well
To consider, how much may slide into hell;
For it seems to your servant singing this hymn,
That the part for the gods is almighty slim.

Friends, I'm a lumberman, and tell what I know,—
That in poor grades there's hell and profits are
   low,—
But we'll find when we get to Jupiter's land,
That the profit in "clears" is almighty grand.

And as we pass through the Arcadian grove
Where all the great gods and fair goddesses rove,
We may be invited to a banquet most grand
Where nectar exalts in that almighty land.

Where Orpheus,—for strains that lingeringly
   dwell,
Doth finger the strings of the enchanted shell;
And for music on high, which ever shall lead,
Old Marsyas doth pipe his almighty reed.

Then may we behold our great Tappan advance,
With proud Juno in hand, to lead in a dance,
And we shall all join the Olympian girls,
And laugh when Jupiter shakes his almighty curls.

Nor will be debarred from that banqueting floor
The girls of our campus, who are read in the lore
Of Homer and Virgil, and passed all our classes,
And have climbed the heights of almighty Par-
   nassus.

"LOOKING BACKWARD"

TO MRS. W. I. WAY, TOPEKA, KANSAS.

The author was asked what he thought of Bellamy's "Looking Backward", and responded as follows: It is the old satyr which Plato in his "Banquet" made Alcibiades liken Socrates to. It is a rude and wanton goat, with horns and cloven hoof, and hairy skin wrapped round a hidden god within, who pipes the heavenly music of Marsyas. I submit the following review as a close imitation in theory and plan of book, but not in diction or subject.

"*Looking Backward!*" I've read the book, —
 It's wearisome and trifling;
It's an old salt, like the leal look
 Of Lot's unsavory wifeling,
  Looking backward.

As I look back to boyhood years,
 Ah! sadly I remember,
The ride I took with my bay steers;
 'T was coldly in December,
  As I look back.

In tumbling leaps old tumblers tip
 For a perspective survey,
Then forward jump and as they flip
 They see things topsy-turvy,
  In tumbling leaps.

Looking Backward.

I was the son of Deacon Cash, —
   Sweet was the preacher's daughter,
And her eyes shone in heaven's flash,
   Like lakes of sparkling water:
     I was the sun.

This looking back is a torn leaf
   From out old Memory's wish-book, —
It is a lie, a cheat, a thief,
   A false fly on the fish hook,
     This looking back.

She was the girl that I loved best,
   Now, since the last September;
And my heart burned beneath my vest,
   Just like a hickory ember, —
     She was the girl.

It touches not the heart in these
   Damp days of solid learning;
We pant for new life, the fresh breeze,
   Wafting some new heart's yearning, —
     It touches not.

Upon the sled away we bore;
   Robes wrapped us up in gladness; —
Heavenly stars! how they ran and tore
   The pure white snow! — white sadness
     Upon the sled.

It is too old for this day's thought; —
Lucretius sleeps with Moses, —
Give us the thing the heart has wrought,
Spellbound with this day's posies: —
It is too old.

Two miles from fire, — then an elm tree
Both steers together straddled; —
'T was lightning struck my girl and me,
And stars and steers skedaddled;
Two miles from fire.

When he looked back on ages past
Grand Plato saw Atlantis;
And More, Utopia wrote at last;
But Bellamy burst their panties,
When he looked back.

There was no trouble in that meeting,
Reaching the heart I treasure;
For soon I found it proudly beating
To mine in rhythmic measure; —
There was no trouble.

If we look back in prose or rhyme,
Why drawl it through the ages?
Give us the fire of present time,
To burnish up the pages,
If we look back.

I love her yet, though far apart, —
　She taught me early teaming, —
I broke my steers, she broke my heart, —
　But there's no harm in dreaming
　　I love her yet.

As age creeps on old fields we glean,
　Bent forward at the gleaning; —
At last we tumble as we lean,
　And Time rakes up with meaning,
　　As age creeps on.

A YOUNG LADY'S HOLOCAUST.

My lover's letters saved with sacred care,
   Tear stained I bring before the welcome fire,
   Inspired by some unholy, fell desire
To burn these missives, once so sweet and fair,
And float their priceless perfumes in the air.
   Now! as they rise upon the funeral pyre,
   And hopes of life and dreams of love expire,
It seems the scent of blossoms still is there.
Dear, darling treasures of my maiden dream!
   The brief, fond flutter of my blooming heart!
O friendly fire, how warm and bright ye gleam!
   As now blind Cupid's trophies here depart.
Henceforth to me how vain and weak shall seem
   The captive chains, and splendors of his dart.

THE CHILD OF FATE.

The child of fate sat on a grassy bank
Of Time's swift stream, and careless said: "My
    plank
I launch, and on this flood I'll reach the *Great!*
I shall be honored of the mighty state,
And I shall rise, and none shall me outrank."
But soon athirst, he of the waters drank,
And into dark forgetfulness he sank—
    And fortune missed—with dreamy senses sate—
        The child of fate.

Then dear, kind Nature came, and seized the crank,
And tore him from his raft, where chains did clank,
    And said: "Arise, before it is too late!"
    And pounded sense and shame into his pate;
And then, with all her energies did spank
        The child of fate.

A SCOTCH SONG: "STORMY WEATHER."

A LASSIE braw had cawd her kye
    Amang the tangled heather;
And aften she would moan and sigh:
    "It's chill and stormy weather;
And I'm alane, and there is nane
    Wi' whom I may forgether;
And aft I greet wi my cauld feet,
    This stoor and stormy weather."

When Jamie lad cam ower the knowe
    She put him in a swither;
As modestly she tauld him how
    She could 'na thole the weather.
He asked her name, and whaur her hame,
    And spiert aboot her father;
But nane she'd name, to tak the blame,
    But cauld and stormy weather.

Then Jamie said: "Come bide wi' me
    While it is stormy weather;
For something tells me in your e'e
    We'll live and love together."
Then he laid doon his plaid and shoon,
    And Love made them a tether;—
He wrapped her roun', and they were soon
    Beyond the stormy weather.

He whispered in her ear while they
  Were warm and sweet thegither,
And said: "You'll niver rue the day
  You drave amang the heather.
You'll be my wife, and thro' our life
  We'll live and love together;
You'll tak my name, and in our hame
  There'll ne'er be stormy weather."

A GERMAN DRINKING SONG.

Oh! peer's goot when I gets full mit enof,
Und foor dot reasons mine beoples I lof;
Und Sunday to der peer-garten I goes,
Mine pelly to fill oop fon head to toes.

CHORUS:

Oh! gif us a glass of peer, boys,
  Gif us a glass of peer.—
Fill oop der stein so white mit foam,
  To stop our song und thirst;—
Gif it to all dose pellies along,
  Alvays not full to burst.

Und mit those days all mine droobles he goes,
Und den mine feelings coom oop, und I grows—
Und I feel so big dot Gott in der sky
Vas not so tall noor so bigger as I.

Und I gits so fool of lof und goot cheer,
Dot religion comes on top of mine peer;—
Und I lof mine brooder so goot dot day,
I gifs to him all mine moneys avay.

Und I lofs his children und schweet frau too,
Fur dot leetle saucy flies, she would shoo
Fon mine peer glass, und alvays my nose,
Und den I calt her mine Vaterland rose.

I hat all der times mine arm rount her vaste
Und I keest her, which vas schweet to my taste;
Und on dot vat did we do und propose?
Vhy! we trink some more peer! vhat you suppose?

"EXIMPT."

O' KELLY he swore, and bejabers he did,—
  That the head of a family he was,
And the buggy he owned, bejabers he said
  Was ontoirly eximpt at the laws.

Fur the raison was clear, bejabers it was,
  That he hauled therein the stuff he ate,
And whisky he drank, when he plead at the laws,
  And rode in, fur the paple to chate.

O' Kelly a farmer, bejabers he was,
  Who leased out his sole acre on shares,
To the big bugs, and the grasshoppers and craws,
  And hauled home therein, bejabers,— *the tares.*

And a granger he was, bejabers he said,
  Before whom he now plead his own cause,—
And fur the above raisons, and other ones hid,
  This buggy, it was eximpt at the laws.

THE LOANED BOOK.

I LOANED her a book, 'twas a beautiful psalm,
The sweet and quaint poem of Omar Khayyam.

From my own hand she took this treasure of
    mine,—
This story of Life, and read line upon line.

What was dark as a dream in figure of speech,
Clear marginal notes the true meaning did teach.

And pure as a brook that runs bright over sand,
And sparkling with truth, was this book from my
    hand.

Alas! not by the hand in which it was placed,
Like some Orient gem her fingers had graced;

But by far other hand the book was returned,
As tho' the hand favored, the favor had spurned.

ALONE.

WHAT sounds of sorrow from the dark inane
Come to the soul that feels itself alone!—
Its only self to hear the lonely groan,
For its lost self, weeping o'er friendships slain,
And flitting faiths that ne'er will come again.
   It is the storm at sea, whose thunder tone
   Dies in the misty cloud or billows' moan,
Weeping its fitful self away in rain.
And I have seen a lone, forsaken bird,
   Whose wonted mate was dead, droop his tired wing,
And wait the call that should no more be heard,—
   Until the storms of Winter past, and Spring
Had budded forth again, some warbled word
Of love attuned again his heart to sing.

THE ENCHANTED GARDEN.

THERE is a garden where I love to dwell,—
   There no rude winds do blow, nor scorching sun
   Shines in upon the work ere it is done;
Nor anything there done too sad to tell;
For there all life is an enchanted spell.
   It is a place where crystal waters run,
   Gurgling through flowery mead which charm-
     eth one
Like the soft chimings of a distant bell.
Within this garden grows the tree which yields
   To man the measure of its fruitful joys;
And in its mighty top and branches shields
   The charmèd inmates that it there decoys;
There all the blushing flowers of virtue start,—
It is the garden of a lovely heart.

SILVER THREADS.

TO MRS. JOHN FARNSWORTH, FORT SCOTT, KANSAS.

How sad the years do beckon back
Our thoughts along Life's beaten track;
   And visions of the long ago
   Float round us as they come and go,
And sacred memories linger there,
When silver threads come in the hair.

And sad the song old Ocean sings,
As homeward he our cargo brings,
   To find our ships were tempest tossed,
   And our fond hopes were sunk and lost,
And promised wealths were buried there,
When silver threads come in the hair.

And sad our souls are bowed in grief,
As we turn over, leaf by leaf,
   The sacred book our lives have made,
   To find therein less light than shade,
And long-lost hearts and faces fair,
When silver threads come in the hair.

Yet sweet it is for us to know,
That flowers do live beneath the snow;
   And Winter always hath its Spring,
   When flowers will bloom and birds will sing;
And souls we love will grow more fair,
When silver threads come in the hair.

WHAT IS THE WORLD TO ME?

What is the world to me without
    One loving heart to cherish;
Who ne'er my faithful love will doubt,
    Though other faiths may perish?—
For it's a phantom flitting past
That says: No faith nor love shall last.

What is the world to me, when no
    Soft lips, with their caressing,
Invite my soul to stay, and go
    Not elsewhere for its blessing?—
For it's no phantom of the air
That makes those lips destroy my care

What is the world to me, when those
    Bright eyes the fairies lend her,
To light my soul to its repose,
    Shine not for me in splendor?—
For 't was a phantom of the mind
That painted Eros young and blind.

What is the world to me, if there
    Be not one fond and certain
To veil me with her silken hair,
    A soft, disheveled curtain?—
For she's no phantom of the night
Who veils my soul in soft delight.

What is the World to Me?

What is the world to me, although
    My praise be world-wide spoken,
Without some one to say, I know
    His pledge was never broken?—
For piping phantoms never voice
That praise which makes my heart rejoice.

What is the world to me, with all
    Its gilded pomp and pleasure,
Without some dearest one to call
    My own, my heart's sweet treasure?
I'll have no phantom in my grasp,
But one soul's wealth of love to clasp!

"THE MAPLES."

Name of my home, at Mound City. Suggested by Mrs. Ella C. Porter.

Ye village of the Maple hills,
    I sing thy song,—
Bowed in the shadows of the past,
    I plaint thy wrong;—
Let every sense that beauty thrills
    Thy praise complete!
For Nature brings her gifts to cast
    Them at thy feet.

Ye Maples of the towering hills
    And flowery glade!
How thy tall trunks and branches cast
    The somber shade!
And while my soul thy beauty thrills,
    Thy shadows creep—
For in the shadows of the past,
    My hopes do sleep.

Dear Maples! now thy shimmering leaves
    For loving kiss,
Turn throbbing to the evening breeze
    With floating bliss.

How oft beneath thy dripping eaves,
 In summer shower,
Have warblers of the summer trees
 Enjoyed thy bower!

How doth my soul the shimmering leaves
 Of Memory kiss!
How oft my heart doth throbbing seize
 The floating bliss!
When baby arms, in snow-white sleeves,
 Did bless the Power
That spread the shadows of the trees,
 For summer hour.

Sweet Maples! Now your saddening shade
 Doth crape my head;
As reverently I.lowly bow
 Unto my dead.
Two sister hearts are lowly laid,
 Both safe and sweet:—
"*The Maples*" cast their shadows now,
 Close to their feet.

HISTORIC NOTES.

NOTE 1.

One of the most memorable expeditions which followed the conquest of Mexico was that led by Francisco Vasquez de Coronado, in search of the seven cities of Cibola and the famed land of Quivira, during the years 1540 to 1542.

It takes us back to a time when but little was known of this western hemisphere, or, in fact, of the size, shape or geography of the earth; to a time when physical science was unknown, save what had come down from Aristotle; to a time when the reason of man, inquiring after the causes of things, founded its speculations on fancy rather than fact. It was just at the dawn of intellectual freedom, ushered in by the invention of printing; and nineteen years before Elizabeth ascended the throne of England, whose reign named an age in letters and science. It was eighty years before Bacon gave to the world his Novum Organum; sixty years before Shakespeare put upon the stage those masterly plays which will outlive his nation; and eighty years before the Pilgrims landed with their story of grief to chant their song of freedom in the American wilderness.

This army which Coronado led out of Mexico, to go with him in quest of gold and to plant the cross on the Rocky Mountains and on the plains of Kansas, contained only three hundred men, but the best and noblest blood of Spain ran in their veins. It is said no other expedition in the new world contained more men of noble birth. Among them we find the resolute Captains Melchior Diaz and Juan de Saldibar, who, with but twelve men as an advance guard, penetrated the primeval wilderness northward seven hundred miles, and afterward, under the direction of Coronado, went in search of and found the records of the adventurer and sailor, Don Fernando

Alarçon, who had ascended the Colorado river 160 miles from its mouth, but who was forced to abandon the expedition at the northern extremity of the Gulf of California. Hernando d'Alvarado was also another great captain, who with small detachments of troops explored the country for many hundreds of miles right and left of Coronado's route. We find also the historians Castañeda and Jaramillo, who accompanied the expedition from beginning to end, and faithfully chronicled its history.

When we consider this small troop of men separating themselves from their companions in arms, and, without any base for supplies, plunging into an unknown wilderness, with its inaccessible mountains, its mighty streams, and treeless, sandy deserts, to there subsist on what the chase or the Indian could bestow, to contend against the vicissitudes of the seasons, the climate and the elements, and to encounter for nearly three years the savage beasts and more savage man, we are overwhelmed with wonder at their daring and fortitude. It reveals to us in no small degree the indomitable pluck and energy, the sturdy and tireless soldiery, and the unbounded zeal which animated those old Spanish cavaliers who fought the battles of Spain under Ferdinand and Isabella and established the power and glory of Charles the Fifth.

NOTE 2.

The immediate cause of Coronado's march was the marvelous story which Alvar Nuñez Cabeça de Vaca told on his arrival in Mexico, after having traveled from east to west across the continent. This celebrated gentleman and historian, whom Robertson calls "one of the most gallant and virtuous of Spanish adventurers," was the treasurer of that ill-fated military expedition undertaken by Narvaez in Florida, in the year 1528. In less than one year this whole command perished, either by the enemy, by starvation, or the elements. Cabeça with three others alone survived. They remained with the natives for six years, near the coast of the Gulf of Mexico, and at last, after having learned the language, the habits and character of the Indian tribes frequenting those parts, they effected their escape. They passed northward into the mountains of Alabama; then taking a northwestern course into Tennessee, were the first white men to discover the Mississippi river, which Cabeça called "*the great river*" coming from the north. This discovery preceded De Soto at least six years. This river they crossed, and traveled westward through northern Arkansas, and up the Arkansas around the great bend. There is no doubt that Cabeça and his companions were the first white men within historic times who had touched upon the soil of Kansas. It is reported by the chroniclers of Coronado's expedition that "ten days after leaving the Rio de Cicuyé," (at a point near the present town of Pecos, on their march,) "they discovered some tents of tanned buffalo skins, inhabited by Indians who were like Arabs, and who were called Querechios, and continuing their march in a northeasterly direction, they soon came to a village which Cabeça de Vaca and Dorantes had passed through on their way from Florida to Mexico."

This village was at least 250 miles from the present town of Pecos, and by the "trail" was certainly in Kansas. This old Indian trail, along which was borne the commerce of prehistoric times, passed just west of the great cañon of the Canadian river, thence through the cities of Cibola into Old Mexico. On this trail Cabeça went thence through New Mexico, passing near Zuñi's heights and southward to Old Mexico, where he arrived in 1536, having been one year on his journey. His report, made up of the story of his bondage, his travels and trials by land and sea, his knowledge of a vast continent which he had traversed, the home of heretofore unknown races of men, all colored in fervid language and imagination, became a great unwritten poem of adventure to Coronado, of which he should become the hero in daring deeds and brilliant exploits.

NOTE 3.

The seven cities of Cibola, instead of being that in number, and instead of being "a great city, inhabited with great store of people, and having streets and market places, and built of certain great houses of five stories high, of lime and stone," turned out to be a few common Pueblo adobes. These structures were composed of dried mud, and were seldom more than one story high, similar in all respects to those of the Tlascans and Tescucans of Mexico at the time of the conquest. J. H. Simpson, in his article on the "Seven Cities of Cibola," (Smithsonian Report, 1869,) says: "In the year 1530, Nuño de Guzman, president of New Spain, was informed by his slave, an Indian from the province of Tejos, situated somewhere north from Mexico, that in his travels he had seen cities so large that they might compare with the City of Mexico; that these cities were seven in number, and had streets that were exclusively occupied by workers in gold and silver; that to reach them a journey of forty days was required, and that travelers penetrated that region by directing their steps northwardly between the two seas." This story proved to be one of the many Indian fables told to the Spanish adventurer for the purpose of exciting or curing his disease —"*the desire for gold.*"

Cibola was never found, for the reason that it never existed. Simpson, above quoted, thinks Zuñi is the spot. He followed the guess of Gallatin, Squier, Whipple, Prof. Turner, and Kern. Others think Chaco the spot; some Santa Fé; while others again hold that the "seven cities" were located far to the eastward. But while these seven cities of Cibola never came to light, the fact remains that many small villages existed in New Mexico and along the Gila river, the habitations of a race of Indians who did not live alone by the chase, but combined with this a rude and primitive agriculture, with some few simple domestic arts. This distinguished them from the wild, Arab-like, roving Indians of the plains, who lived in movable tents made of tanned buffalo skins.

The Pueblos also dug caves into the sides of the mountains at places, which proved a means of defense against their roving neighbors, and with whom they came in contact on the great plains, the home of the buffalo. In these caves and mud villages they dwelt for ages, comparatively secure, yet in disgusting primitive filth and squalor.

The fabulous stories told by the Indians were only equaled by the Spaniard's contempt of truth in relating his exploits in the new world. The fables of the Indian became a jack-o'-lantern to the chivalrous Spaniard, which he followed from place to place. Not to be outdone when he found himself duped, he often reported as veritable great adventures which he had undertaken, in a vast empire filled with magnificent cities, and inhabited by a powerful, rich and brave people, and who at last were subdued by his valor. It is indeed pleasant for the honest searcher after historic truth to get down from the dizzy heights of story to which Irving and Prescott have led him, and to tread the solid and stubborn ground of fact with such a student as R. A. Wilson, and other historic and scientific workers in our own practical age.

NOTE 4.

It cannot be denied that the soldiers of Coronado's army, though principally of high birth, were sadly disappointed at the disgusting spectacle of Pueblo women living in their unparalleled filth and brutality; for in all the expeditions of adventure by the conquering Spaniard in New Spain the soldier looked forward with lustful hope, as much to share the captured Indian damsel, as to the precious metals or brilliant stones of the earth. The leaders themselves shared and set the example of this primitive lustful luxury. Don Pedro d'Alvarado had under Cortes, at the fall of the Tlascan republic, received an Indian beauty, Donna Louisa, the daughter of a chief; and five other Indian girls were apportioned to other officers, says Prescott, "after they had been cleansed from the stains of infidelity by the waters of baptism," Cortes himself lived in the constant companionship of Donna Marina, who, "beautiful as a goddess," served him as mistress and interpreter, from the time he captured her at Tobasco, till after the conquest. While threading his way through the everglades of Honduras, and contemplating his return to Spain, he gave this faithful friend to Don Juan Xamorillo, a Castilian knight. As soon as her services become no longer profitable she is with trifling ceremony discarded, and her name disappears from history.

In connection with this Spanish brutality and lust, Diaz, (vol. 1, p. 368,) says: "After peace had been restored to the old province, and the inhabitants had submitted to his majesty, Cortes, finding there was nothing to be done at present, determined with the crown officers to mark all the slaves with the iron. . . . On the night preceding, the finest of the Indian females had been secretly set apart, so that when it came to a division among the soldiers, we find none left but old and ugly women. . . . A soldier asked Cortes if the division of gold in Mexico was not a sufficient imposition; and now he was going to deprive the poor soldiers, who had undergone so many hardships, and suffered from innumerable wounds, of this small remuneration, and not even allow him a pretty Indian female for a companion.

NOTE 5.

"Il Turco," (*the Turk*,) says Castañeda, the historian of Coronado's march, "was an Indian slave, a native of the country on the side of Florida." Florida was that undefined country which extended from Canada to the Rio del Norte, and included the great basin of the Mississippi. The Turk told Coronado that in his country there was a river two leagues broad, and that it was beyond the province of Quivira. This was undoubtedly the Mississippi. The story he told to induce the Spaniard to leave the Pueblo country was a mixture of fact and fiction; and would impose on no one but the most credulous. It was this: "That in his country there was a river two leagues broad, in which were fish as large as horses; that there were canoes with twenty oarsmen on each side and which were also propelled by sails; that the lords of the land were seated in their sterns upon a dais, while a large golden eagle was affixed to the prows; that the sovereign of the land took his siesta beneath a huge tree, to whose branches golden bells were hung, which were rung by the agitation of the summer breeze; that the commonest vessels were of sculptured silver, and that the bowls, plates and dishes were of gold." Coronado says he was told that the king of Quivira had a long beard, was hoary-headed and rich. In his report to Mendoça, on his return, he says: "The tale they (the guides) told me then, that Quivira was a city of extraordinary buildings and full of gold, was false. In inducing me to part with all my army to come to this country, the Indians thought that the country being desert and without water they would conduct us into places where our horses and ourselves would die of hunger; that is what the guides confessed. They told that they had acted by the advice of the natives of these countries." In all probability, "Il Turco" was neither a slave of the Pueblos nor an inhabitant of the Mississippi, but one of their wisest and bravest men. In him we witness the unconquerable spirit, that self abnegation and abandon, which is so prominent in the Indian character, and was so many times exhibited in their dealings with the Spanish conquerers. This action of *the Turk* was neither new nor strange; it had often been enacted before. The false story he told, the crafty duplicity with which he entered into all the minutiæ of the plot, the religious zeal with which it was undertaken, the masterly skill with which it was executed, the frankness with which he avowed the object and cause of the deception when the journey was completed, and that firmness and fearlessness with which he met death, portray one of the grandest attributes of the Indian character. We see the same story told and the same acts performed in the wilds of Panama, when the cacique Uracca betrayed d'Avila; and in the everglades of Florida, when "Pedro" led De Soto after the vain illusion of gold into the pathless and almost impenetrable wilderness.

NOTE 6.

The place where the red pipe stone is found, or the pipe stone from which the pipe of peace is made, is now definitely located in the southwestern county of Minnesota. This pipe stone was an article of commerce with the North American Indians from time immemorial. It was held sacred by them, and the place where it was obtained was holy ground. Pipes of this stone have been found in graves which were made by men at a time contemporaneous with the extinct mastodon. (Smithsonian Report, 1882, pp. 690-713.)

Charles Rau, in his essay on "Ancient Aboriginal Trade in North America," says: "The celebrated red pipe stone, that highly-valued material, employed by the Indians of past and present times in the manufacture of their calumets, occurs *in situ* on the Coteau de Prairies, an elevation extending between the Missouri and the headwaters of the Mississippi. This is the classical ground of the surrounding tribes, and many legends lend a romantic interest to that region. It was here that the Great Spirit assembled the various Indian nations and instructed them in the art of making pipes of peace, as related by Longfellow in his charming "Song of Hiawatha." Even hostile tribes met here in peace, for this district was by common consent regarded as neutral ground, where strife and feuds were suspended, that all might resort unmolested to the quarry and supply themselves with the much-prized stone. This material, though compact, is not hard, and therefore easily worked, and, moreover, capable of a high polish. It consists chiefly of silica and alumina, with an admixture of iron which produces the red color. American, and probably also European mineralogists, call this stone catlinite, in honor of the zealous ethnologist and painter, Catlin, who was first to give an accurate account of its place of occurrence, and to relate the traditions connected with the red pipe stone quarry. This locality is the only one in North America where this peculiar stone is found, and it is doubtful indeed whether in any other place on both hemispheres a mineral substance is met which corresponds in every respect to the one in question."

NOTE 7.

"A wide and extensive commerce was carried on between the different nations of this continent, dating back into prehistoric times. We find in a single locality, at Naples, Illinois, "a shell from Florida, obsidian from Mexico, lead ore from Wisconsin or Missouri, copper from Lake Superior, and mica from the Alleghanies;" and this at a time so distant that all computation is out of the question. The Santa Fé trail may be ten thousand years old. Within historic times the Indians of

New York have given battle to their foes on the banks of the Mississippi, and the tribes of Wisconsin have gone to war with their ancient enemies at the foot of the Rocky Mountains in New Mexico, and returned home before the summer was over." (Charles Rau, Smithsonian Report, 1872.)

NOTE 8.

The Spanish historian Gomara describes the buffalo as seen by Coronado thus: "These oxen are of the color and bigness of our bulls, but their horns are not so great. They have a great bunch upon their fore shoulders, and more hair upon their fore part than on their hinder part, and it is like wool. They have, as it were, a horse mane upon their back bone, and much hair and very long from the knees downward. They have great tufts of hair hanging down from their foreheads, and it seemeth they have beards, because of the great store of hair hanging down at their chins and throats. The males have very long tails, and a great knob or flock at the end, so that in some respects they resemble lions, and in some others the camel. They push with their horns, they run, they overtake and kill a horse when they are in their rage and anger. Finally, it is a fierce beast of countenance and form of body. The horses fled from them, either because of their deformed shape, or else because they had never seen them. Their masters have no other riches nor substance; of them they eat, they drink, they apparel, they shoe themselves; and of their hides they make many things, as houses, shoes, apparel and ropes; of their bones they make bodkins; of their sinews and hair, thread; of their horns, maws and bladders, vessels; of their dung, fire; of their calf skins, buckets, wherein they draw and keep water. To be short, they make so many things of them as they have need of, or as may suffice in the use of this life."

As to the antiquity of the buffalo, we find him at home with the extinct mastodon of the age of the mound builders, in Dakota and Wisconsin, and his teeth have been found in the drift of Maine. (Smithsonian Rep. 1871, p. 394; Lapham's Antiq. of Wis., and Amer. Naturalist, vol. 1, p. 268, note.) But it must not be forgotten, in this connection, that Cabeça was the first to describe the buffalo.

NOTE 9.

"The guides conducted the general to Quivira in forty-eight days, for they had traveled too much in the direction of Florida. At Quivira they found neither gold nor silver, and learning from the Turk that he had, at the instance of the people of Cicuyé, purposely decoyed the army far into the plains, to kill the horses and thus make the men helpless and fall an easy prey to the natives, and that all he had said about the great quantity of silver and gold to be found there was false, they strangled him." (Castañeda's Relations—Ternaux Compans.)

NOTE 10.

This has reference to the Mandan Indians, a peculiar race, who at the time of Coronado's march must have inhabited the region of country at or near the red pipe stone quarries. (See note 6, *ante*.) Hale, speaking of this race, says: "They had a decided superiority over any of the other western tribes in the arts of domestic life. Their pottery was quite convenient, and they relied without fear upon their crops of corn, squashes and pumpkins. They did not make war unless attacked, but fortified their positions with skill and care. They presented an additional peculiarity in the frequent whiteness of their skin and light color of their hair. Many of them who are full-blooded have beautiful white complexions. The differences in the color of hair are as great as in complexions; for in a numerous group of these people, and more particularly among the females, who never take pains to change its natural color as the men often do, there may be seen every shade of color of hair, with the exception of red or auburn, which is not to be found; and it is a strange peculiarity that there are very many natives of both sexes, and of every age, from infancy to manhood and old age, with hair of a bright silvery gray, and in some instances almost perfectly white." (Hale's "Kansas and Nebraska," pp. 30–40.) It was undoubtedly this Mandan race that Turco had in his mind when he told Coronado that "the king of

Quivira had long beard, was hoary-headed and rich." He certainly led Coronado in the direction of the habitation of the Mandan people. Mr. Catlin, who spent much time with them, believes they descended from the Madoc colony of Welch, and gives many cogent reasons therefor. (Hale's "Kansas and Nebraska," pp. 31, 32.) They migrated at an early day, descended the Ohio river, and ascended the Missouri, and perished as a race near its head waters, within the last thirty years.

Robert Southey founded his poem "Madoc" on the story of this Welch colony, which came to America in the twelfth century, and which I give from Hakluyt's "Voyage," as follows: "Madoc, another of Owen Guinneth's sons, left the land in contention between his brethren, and prepared certain ships with men and amunition and sought adventures by sea, sailing west and leaving the coast of Ireland so far south that he came to land unknown, where he saw many strange things. This land must needs be part of that country of which the Spaniards affirm themselves to be the first finders since Honna's time. . Of the voyage and return of Madoc there be many fables formed, as the common people do use in distance of place and length of time, rather to augment than diminish; *but sure it is that there he was.* And after he had returned home and declared the pleasant and fruitful countries that he had seen without inhabitants, and on the contrary, part for what wild and barren ground his brothers and nephews did murther one another, he prepared a number of ships, and got with him such men and women as were desirous to live in quietness, and taking leave of his friends, took his journey northward again. Therefore it is to be presupposed that he and his people inhabited part of those countries. . . . But because this people were not many they followed the manners of the land and used the language they found there. This Madoc arriving in that western country, into which he came in the year 1170, left most of his people there and returning back for more of his own nation, acquaintances and friends to inhabit that fair and large country, went thither again with ten sails, as I find noted by Gutyn Owen." Thus says Hakluyt, who wrote in the time of Queen Elizabeth. That this country was visited by the maritime adventurers of Europe, Africa and Asia long before Columbus and long before the Christian era, there seems reason no longer to dispute. That the civilization of Central America, not as exhibited by the inhabitants at the time of the conquest, but as portrayed in its vast ruins, its obelisks, paintings, hieroglyphic tablets and plinths, its sepulchers, crosses, temples and emblems, points to a Phœnician origin, is rendered almost certain. (Wilson's History of the Conquest of Mexico.) If then this be true, the story of Madoc certainly comes within historic probability; and the physical and mental peculiarities of the Mandan people, as exhibited in their domestic and warlike habits, are thus easily accounted for.

NOTE 11.

That Coronado passed easterly through Kansas, is established beyond controversy. The problem is, to define the route traveled with probable certainty. This can only be done from what Coronado and his historians tell us. Coronado describes Quivira, in his report to the viceroy, Mendoça, as follows:

"The province of Quivira is 930 leagues (3,240 miles) from (the city of) Mexico. The place I have reached is the fortieth degree of latitude. The earth is the best possible for all kinds of productions of Spain, for while it is very strong and black, it is very well watered by brooks, springs and rivers. I found prunes like those of Spain, some of which were black; also some excellent grapes and mulberries. I sojourned twenty-five days in the province of Quivira, as much to thoroughly explore the country as to see if I could not find some further occasion to serve your majesty, for the guides whom I brought with me have spoken of provinces situated still further on. That which I have been able to learn is, that in all this country one can find neither gold nor any other metal. They spoke to me of small villages, whose inhabitants for the most part do not cultivate the soil. They have huts of hides and willows, and change their places of abode with the vaches (buffaloes)." (Coronado's

Historic Notes. 155

Relations — Ternaux Compans; Smithsonian Report, 1869; p. 338, note.)

Jaramillo, a companion of the expedition, says: "This country has a superb appearance, and such that I have not seen better in all Spain; neither in Italy nor France, nor in any other country where I have been in the service of your majesty. It is not a country of mountains; there are only some hills, some plains, and some streams of very fine water. It satisfied me completely. I presume that it is very fertile, and favorable for the cultivation of all kinds of fruits."

And Castañeda, the historian of Quivira, says: "It is in this country that the *Espiritu Sancto* (Mississippi river), which Don Fernando de Soto discovered in Florida, takes its source."

In this connection it must be remembered that "Florida" embraced the whole Mississippi basin, and that in Coronado's march he was led by the guides "too far in the direction of Florida."

To determine the course of Coronado's march, its direction and distance, consult Simpson's Smithsonian Report, 1871. In this connection I quote the language of J. H. Simpson, Smithsonian Report, 1869, page 337. After canvassing the whole matter, he says: "No; I am of the opinion that Coronado and his army marched just as Castañeda, Jaramillo and Coronado have reported; that is, generally in a northeast direction, over extensive plains, through countless herds of buffalo and prairie dog villages, and at length, after getting in a manner lost, and finding, as the chronicler says, they had gone "too far towards Florida," that is, to the eastward, and had traveled from Tignex for thirty-seven days, or a distance of between 700 and 800 miles, their provisions failing them, the main body turned back to Tiguex, and Coronado with thirty-six picked men continued his explorations northwardly to the fortieth degree of latitude, where he reached a province which the Indians called Quivira."

At what point in Kansas did Coronado send his army back? It can only be approximated. The army returned "by the arrow," that is, in nearly a straight line. They took some Indian guides, called "Teyans," a nomadic nation, perhaps Kan-

sas Indians, "who knew the country perfectly well," and
"every morning they watched to note where the sun rose, and
directed their way by shooting an arrow in advance, and then
before reaching this arrow they discharged another. In this
way they marked the whole of their route to the spot where
water was to be found and where they encamped." On this
route they passed through the salt marshes on the Canadian,
and this is one point we fix; the other known point is about
130 miles east of Pecos, on the Colorado, where Fort Bascom
is now laid down on the map. To reach this point on the out-
ward journey the army traveled, says the historian, 250 leagues,
or 850 miles, from Tiguex, now Socorro, New Mexico. As the
Indian guides took Coronado's army into the wilderness to kill
it, they most probably followed the line indicated by Simpson,
which would cover about 800 miles. From this point at which
the army returned, Coronado took thirty horsemen and six foot
soldiers, and in eleven days reached Quivira. On his route
he crossed a large river, which they named St. Peter and
St. Paul. After he had reached Quivira, the guides told him
of a still larger river, the "Espiritu Sancto" (Mississippi),
further on to the east. Quivira was therefore in northeastern
Kansas. Coronado remained in Quivira twenty-five days, and
on his return, says the historian, Castañedo: "Notwithstanding
he had good guides, and was not encumbered with baggage,
Coronado was forty days in making the journey from Quivira."
This was at least 1,000 miles from Socorro. In fact, there is
no testimony to show a less number of miles traveled than is
here indicated.

NOTE 12.

"The blue-eyed maid Tritonian Pallas, fierce,
Rousing the war field's tumult, unsubdued,
Leader of armies, awful, whose delight
The shout of battle and the shock of war."
—*Hesiod.*

NOTE 13.

The advent of Columbia, the genius of American civiliza-
tion, the goddess who is supposed to preside over the destinies

of our Republic, has not heretofore been honored with a genealogy, nor has her advent been sung. The author has followed Hesiod for her maternal ancestry, and has connected her with the Grecian hierarchy. (See Hesiod's Theogony.)

NOTE 14.

"Kansas the name; child of the wind." Andreas, in his History of Kansas, says: "Kausas means smoky, in the language of the tribe." He copied from writers Holloway and others, who must have known little or nothing of the history or language of these Indians, or cognate tribes. Perhaps the best authority in the world in regard to the meaning of the word Kansas is the Rev. J. Owen Dorsey, of the bureau of ethnology in the Smithsonian Institution, at Washington. He is certainly very high authority, from his long association with and his extensive studies in the language and history of the Siouan tribes. He says: "While the exact meaning of Kansas is unknown to me, I am sure it does not mean 'smoky, in the language of the tribe.' That would be cúdjujü´, filled with smoke; or else, cúdje égu, smoke-like. . . . The old spelling of Long and others, Konza, is nearer to the original name than is our Kansas. It (Konza) is almost the pronunciation of Kan-ze, the tribal name. Omaha and Quapaw are names of comparatively modern origin, having been given when the people separated at the mouth of the Ohio river. They are correlatives (up-stream people and down-stream people) — geographical names. But Kan-ze, Pañka and Waçaçe (or Kansas), Ponka and Osage are very ancient names, whose true meanings are not revealed outside of the secret society of the tribes. These are mythical or sacred names. Ponka is associated with the red cedar, and Kansas with the wind. . . . The Omaha Mau-ze gens (or clan) has wind names for its males and females. The corresponding Kansas gens is the Kau-ze, part of whom are wind people, or south-wind people. The corresponding Osage gens has several names, Kau-se, etc., meaning south-wind people." (Letter to author, dated July 20, 1886.) The same writer, under date of August 12, 1886, says: "I maintain the following:

1. Kansas does not mean, nor has it meant, in the language of the Kansas or Kaw tribe, nor in that of any cognate tribe, as far as I have ascertained, smoky. 2. Kansas, in one form or another, is at present — and this must have been the case for hundreds of years — applied in the Omaha, Kansas and Osage tribes to gentes or parts of which are said to be wind people. 3. Kan-s̩e, Kan-ze, Ṁau-ze should not be confounded with An-sage, K'an-sage, etc. (swift). The rule is, that difference of sound makes difference of meaning."

NOTE 15.

On the 30th of May, 1854, President Pierce signed the Kansas-Nebraska bill.

NOTE 16.

The doctrine or principle upon which the Southern Confederacy was founded, at the time of secession, is, that *slavery is right;* that it is a great physical, philosophical and moral truth, and especially the natural and normal condition of the negro. Shortly after the government of the Confederate States of America was organized, its vice president, A. H. Stevens, in a speech at Savannah, said: "The new constitution has put to rest forever all the agitating questions relating to our peculiar institutions — African slavery as it exists among us — the proper status of the negro in our form of civilization. This was the immediate cause of the late rupture and present revolution. Jefferson, in his forecast, had anticipated this as the rock upon which the old Union would split. . . . The prevailing ideas entertained by him and most of the leading statesmen, at the time of the formation of the old constitution were, that the enslavement of the African was in violation of the laws of nature; that it was wrong in principle, socially, morally and politically. Our new government is founded upon *exactly the opposite idea;* its foundations are laid, its corner stone rests, upon the *great truth*, that the negro is not equal to the white man; *that slavery*, subordination to the superior race, *is his natural and normal condition.* This, our new government, is the first in the world based upon this great physical, philosophical and moral truth." (Am. Cy., 1861, p. 128.)

Judge Jeremiah S. Black, the eminent jurist, says: "My faith and my reason both assure me that the infallible God proceeded on good grounds when he authorized slavery in Judea." (N. A. Review, August, 1881.)

I quote the above to show at this time what the younger generation has perhaps overlooked in its study of the civil war. The above doctrine of Alexander II. Stevens was the full-fledged political faith of the Southrons who invaded Kansas in 1854-6. But this great *"moral truth"* of the South could not long endure under the civilization of the nineteenth century.

Abraham Lincoln, in his Cooper Institute speech, February 27, 1860, speaking of the demands of the South, said: "Holding, as they do, that slavery is morally right and socially elevating, they cannot cease to demand a full national recognition of it as a legal right and a social blessing. Nor can we justifiably withhold this on any ground save our conviction that slavery is wrong. If slavery is right, all words, acts, laws and constitutions against it are themselves wrong, and should be silenced and swept away. If it is right, we cannot justly object to its nationality, its universality; if it is wrong, they cannot justly insist upon its extension, its enlargement. All they ask we could readily grant, if we thought slavery right; all we ask they could readily grant, if they thought it wrong. Their thinking it right, and our thinking it wrong, is the precise fact upon which depends the whole controversy."

This controversy was at last ended by the civil war, and the "precise fact" whether slavery was right or wrong was decided at the point of the bayonet under the flag of the Union. In this connection we may remark of Truth, in passing, that "the eternal years of God are hers."

NOTE 17.

As soon as the Kansas-Nebraska act was signed and made known, the inhabitants of Missouri took possession of Kansas, and determined to make slavery the corner stone of her political edifice. To this end they came into Leavenworth county, passed the following resolutions, and returned to their homes: "That we will afford protection to no Abolitionist as a settler of this Territory. That we recognize the institution of slavery as already existing in this Territory, and advise slaveholders to introduce their property as early as possible." (Kansas Affairs, p. 2.) These resolutions certainly foreshadowed the Dred-Scott decision, and preceded it three years.

In this connection Dr. Gihon, secretary to Governor Geary, says: "It (slavery) resolved, as a matter of safety and interest, not only to disperse those (Free-State immigrants) who had already entered the Territory, but to prevent, if possible, the admission of all others of similar character. To this end meetings were held in various parts of the Territory and in the border towns of Missouri, at which speeches were made and resolutions adopted of the most incendiary and inflammatory description. At one of these meetings, held at Westport, Mo., in July, 1854, an association was formed, and adopted the following resolutions:

"'*Resolved*, That this association will, whenever called upon by any of the citizens of Kansas Territory, hold itself in readiness together to assist to remove any and all emigrants who go there under the auspices of the Northern Emigrant Aid Society.

"'*Resolved*, That we recommend to the citizens of other counties, particularly those bordering on the Kansas territory, to adopt regulations similar to those of this association, and to indicate their readiness to operate in the objects of this resolution.'" (Gihon's History of Kansas, p. 29.)

NOTE 18.

"Ruffian" was a word applied by the ruffian to himself. "Let it not be understood that this term 'Border Ruffian' is considered by those to whom it is applied as one of reproach. On the contrary, they boast of it, are proud of it, and do all in their power to merit it, and very many of them have been eminently successful. In their manners they assume the character of the ruffian, in their dress they exhibit the appearance of the ruffian, and in their conversation they labor to convey the inference that they are indeed ruffians.

Historic Notes.

"On the levee at Kansas City stood a sort of omnibus, or wagon, used to convey passengers to and from Westport, upon either side of which was painted, in flaming capitals, the words, 'BORDER RUFFIAN.'

"Imagine a man standing, in long boots covered with dust and mud, drawn over his trousers, the latter made of coarse, fancy-colored cloth, well soiled; the handle of a large bowie knife projecting from one or both boot tops; a leathern belt buckled around his waist, on each side of which is fastened a large revolver; a red or blue shirt, with a heart, anchor, eagle, or some other favorite device, braided on the breast and back, over which is swung a rifle or carbine, a sword dangling by his side; an old slouched hat, with a cockade or brass star on the front or side, and a chicken, goose or turkey feather sticking in the top; hair, uncut and uncombed, covering his neck and shoulders; an unshaved face and unwashed hands—imagine such a specimen of humanity, who can swear any given number of oaths in any specified time; drink any quantity of bad whisky without getting drunk, and boast of having stolen a half dozen horses, and killed one or more Abolitionists, and you will have a pretty fair conception of a border ruffian as he appears in Missouri and in Kansas." (Gihon, pp. 106, 107.)

NOTE 19.

The committee appointed by the lower house of Congress to investigate the *Kansas affairs*, in 1855–56, on which committee was John Sherman, of Ohio, speaking of the secret organizations to establish slavery in Kansas, say: "It was known by different names, such as 'Social Band,' 'Friends' Society,' 'Blue Lodge,' 'The Sons of the South.' Its members were bound together by secret oaths, and they had passwords, signs and grips by which they were known to each other. It embraced great numbers of citizens of Missouri, and was extended into the slave States and into the Territory. Its avowed purpose was not only to extend slavery into Kansas, but also into other territory of the United States, and to form a union of all the friends of the institution. Its plan of operating was to organize and send men *to vote* at the elections in the Territory, to collect money to pay their expenses, and, if necessary, to protect them in voting. This dangerous society was controlled by men who avowed their purpose to extend slavery into the Territory at all hazards, and was altogether the most effective instrument in organizing the subsequent armed invasions and forays. In its lodges in Missouri the affairs of Kansas were discussed; the force necessary to control the elections was divided into bands, and leaders selected; means were collected and signs and badges were agreed upon." (Kansas Affairs, p. 3.) November 16, 1854, the St. Louis *Democrat* says; "Senator Atchison is at present engaged in the upper country banding a secret society of five thousand persons. These, according to rumor, are pledged to move into Kansas on the day of the first election to vote slavery into that Territory." (Wilder's Annals.)

NOTE 20.

At the election held March 30, 1855, for members of the first territorial Legislature, the Missourians came over in hordes, and took control of nearly all the election precincts. The report on Kansas affairs says: "They said if the judges appointed by the Governor did not receive their votes they would choose other judges. Some of them voted several times, changing their hats or coats and coming up to the window again. Some of them claimed a right to vote under the organic act, from the fact that their mere presence in the Territory constituted them residents, though they were from Missouri and had their homes in Missouri. Others said they had a right to vote because Kansas belonged to Missouri, and the people from the East had no right to settle in the Territory and vote there. They said they came to the Territory to elect a Legislature to suit themselves, as the people of the Territory and persons from the East and North wanted to elect a Legislature that would not suit them. Col. Young said he wanted citizens to vote in order to give the election some show of fairness. The Missourians said there would be no difficulty if the citizens did not interfere with their voting; but they were determined to vote; peaceably if they could, but vote anyhow. They said each one of them was prepared for eight rounds without loading, and would go to the ninth round with the butcher knife." (Kansas Affairs, p. 12.) The Legislature was elected in this clandestine manner which gave Kansas the "*Bogus Laws*" of 1855. This consummation brought on the Kansas war, which at last ended in the triumph of freedom.

NOTE 21.

An eminent author and lady of Kansas writes as follows: "The following from the Leavenworth *Herald* will suffice to show the character of the leaders of the Pro-Slavery party and their institution, regarding the manner in which Kansas was to be made a slave State. The plan of operation was laid down in an address to a crowd at St. Joseph, Mo., by Stringfellow: 'I tell you to mark every scoundrel among you that is the least tainted with free-soilism or abolitionism, and exterminate him. Neither give nor take quarter from the d—d rascals. To those having qualms of conscience as to violating laws, State or National, the time has come when such impositions must be disregarded, as your lives and property are in danger; and I advise you, one and all, to enter every election district in Kansas, in defiance of Reeder and his vile myrmidons, and vote at the point of the bowie knife and revolver. What right has Governor Reeder to rule Missourians in Kansas? His proclamation and prescribed oath must be disregarded. It is your interest to do so. Mind that slavery is established where it is not prohibited.'" (Mrs. Robinson's "Kansas," pp. 14–16.)

This, again, is the doctrine of the Dred-Scott decision, and preceded it more than a year. Chief Justice Taney was at this time seventy-eight years old, and was enjoying a ripe old dotage. Doubtless Stringfellow's speech was taken by him to be good law.

"July 20, 1854, a meeting in western Missouri resolves to remove any and all emigrants who go to Kansas under the auspices of the Northern emigrant aid societies."

"October 4, 1854, E. D. Ladd writes to the Milwaukee *Sentinel* that within a few days the Missourians have taken down and moved the tents of our squatters, and burned the cabins while the owners were absent at work." (Wilder's Annals.)

NOTE 22.

At a public indignation meeting held in Leavenworth May 3d, 1855, it was, among other things —

"*Resolved*, To the peculiar friends of northern *fanatics* we say, this is not your country; go home and vent your treason where you will find your sympathy.

"*Resolved*, That we invite the inhabitants of every State, north, south, east and west, to come among us and cultivate the beautiful prairie lands of our Territory, but leave behind you the fanaticism of the *higher law* and all kindred doctrines. Come only to maintain the laws as they exist, and not preach your higher duties of setting them at naught; for we warn you in advance that our institutions are sacred to us and must and shall be respected.

"*Resolved*, That the institution of slavery is known and recognized in this Territory; that we repel the doctrine that it is a moral and political evil, and we hurl back with scorn upon its slanderous authors the charge of inhumanity; and we warn all persons not to come to our own peaceful firesides to slander us and sow seeds of discord between the master and the servant; for much as we may deprecate the necessity to which we may be driven, we cannot be responsible for the consequences.

"*Resolved*, That a vigilance committee consisting of thirty members shall now be appointed, who shall observe and report all such persons as shall openly act in violation of *law and order*, and by the expression of abolition sentiments produce disturbance to the quiet of the citizens or danger of their domestic relations; and all such persons so offending *shall be notified and made to leave the Territory*." (Kansas Affairs, pp. 967, 968.

The following is a duplicate of the notice served on William Phillips, a lawyer of Leavenworth city, a few days prior to the above meeting, pursuant to resolutions adopted:

LEAVENWORTH CITY, April 30, 1855.

SIR —At a meeting of the citizens of Leavenworth and vicinity, we, the undersigned, were appointed a committee to inform you that they have unanimously determined that you must leave this Territory by two o'clock of Thursday next. Take due notice thereof, and act accordingly.

To WILLIAM PHILLIPS." [Signed by ten.]
(Kansas Affairs, p. 906.)

NOTE 23.

The *Squatter Sovereign*, published at Atchison, by Dr. John H. Stringfellow, says: "We can tell the impertinent scoundrels of the *Tribune* that they may exhaust an ocean of ink, their emigrant aid societies spend their millions and billions, their representatives in congress *spout* their heretical theories till doomsday, and his excellency, Franklin Pierce, appoint Abolitionist after Free-Soiler as our Governor, *yet we will continue to lynch and hang*, to tar and feather and drown, every white-livered Abolitionist who dares to pollute our soil."

Hon. S. N. Wood, who had moved into Kansas as early as July 4, 1854, gives us the definition of a "white-livered Abolitionist," in the language of the Missouri squatter. He says: "The Pro-Slavery men from Missouri had met in Kansas, and adopted a code of squatter laws, and the whole Territory seemed staked into claims. They had a register of claims, with an office at Westport, Mo. One law of this remarkable code provided that Nebraska was for the North and Kansas for the South. One provision was, that every white-livered Abolitionist who dared to set foot in Kansas should be hung, and that there might be no mistake, they added: 'Every man north of Mason's and Dixon's line is an Abolitionist.'" (Quarter-Centennial Address.)

NOTE 24.

The following was adopted at a meeting held in Clay county, Missouri, in May, 1855:

"That we regard the efforts of the northern division of the Methodist Episcopal Church to establish itself in our State as a violation of her *plighted faith*, and pledged, as its ministers must be, to the anti-slavery principles of that church, we are forced to regard them as enemies to our institutions. We therefore fully concur with our friends in Platte county in resolving to permit no persons belonging to the Northern Methodist Church to preach in our county." (Gihon, p. 36.)

NOTE 25.

The following is the *Squatter Sovereign's* relation of this affair. It occurred August 16, 1855:

"On Thursday last one Pardee Butler arrived in town, with a view of starting for the East, probably for the purpose of getting a fresh supply of Free-Soilers from the penitentiaries and pest holes of the Northern States. Finding it inconvenient to depart before morning, he took lodging at the hotel, and proceeded to visit numerous portions of our town, everywhere avowing himself a Free-Soiler, and preaching the foulest of abolition heresies. He declared the recent action of our citizens in regard to J. W. B. Kelly, [who was beaten by a mob, and driven from Atchison,] the infamous and unlawful proceedings of a mob, at the same time stating that many persons in Atchison who were Free-Soilers at heart had been intimidated thereby, and feared to avow their true sentiments, but that he would express his views in defiance of the whole community.

"On the ensuing morning our townsmen assembled *en masse*, and deeming the presence of such persons highly detrimental to the safety of our slave property, appointed a committee of two to wait on Mr. Butler, and request his signature to the resolutions passed at the late Pro-Slavery meeting held in Atchison. After perusing the said resolutions, Mr. B. positively declined signing them, and was instantly arrested by the committee.

"After the various plans for his disposal had been considered, it was finally decided to place him on a raft, composed of two logs firmly lashed together; that his baggage and a loaf of bread be given him; and having attached a flag to his primitive bark, emblazoned with mottoes indicative of our contempt of such characters, Mr. Butler was set adrift in the great Missouri, with the letter "R" legibly painted on his forehead. He was escorted some distance down the river by several of our citizens, who, seeing him pass several rock heaps in quite a skillful manner, bade him adieu, and returned to Atchison.

"Such treatment may be expected by all scoundrels visiting our town for the purpose of interfering with our time-honored institutions, and the same punishment we will be happy to award all Free-Soilers, Abolitionists, and their emissaries."

Butler states that Robert S. Kelley, the junior editor of the *Squatter Sovereign,* was one of the most active members of the mob; that he committed this disgraceful act, and that he assisted to tow the raft out into the stream, where he was set adrift, with flags having the following strange inscriptions: "Eastern Emigrant Aid Express — the Rev. Mr. Butler for the Underground Railroad;" "The Way They Are Served in Kansas;" "For Boston;" "Cargo Insured, Unavoidable Danger of the Missourians and the Missouri River Excepted;" "Let Future Emissaries from the North Beware — Our Hemp Crop is Sufficient to Reward All Such Scoundrels."

Mr. Butler also states: "They threatened to shoot me if I pulled my flag down. I pulled it down, cut the flag off the flagstaff, made a paddle of the flagstaff, and ultimately got ashore about six miles below. They all admitted when we were together that I was not an Abolitionist, but a Free-Soiler. By Free-Soiler I mean one in favor of making Kansas a free State." (Kansas Affairs, p. 963.)

NOTE 26.

"On the 21st day of November, 1855, F. M. Coleman, a Pro-Slavery man, and Charles W. Dow, a Free-State man, had a dispute about the division line between their respective claims. Several hours afterward, as Dow was passing from a blacksmith shop towards his claim and by the cabin of Coleman, the latter shot Dow with a double-barrel shot gun, loaded with slugs. Dow was unarmed. He fell across the road and died immediately. This was about one o'clock, and his dead body was allowed to lie where it fell till after sundown." (Kansas Affairs, p. 59.)

This was the immediate cause of the Wakarusa war. (See note 32.)

NOTE 27.

Among those ordered to leave the Territory was Mr. Wm. Phillips, a lawyer, of Leavenworth, who had signed a protest against the election of March 30, in that city. (For protest, see Kansas Affairs, p. 503.) Upon his refusal to go, he was, on the 17th of May, 1855, seized by a band of men, chiefly from Missouri, who carried him eight miles up the river to Weston, where they shaved one-half of his head, tarred and feathered him, rode him on a rail and sold him at a mock auction by a negro, and bid in by another negro for one dollar, all of which he bore with manly fortitude and bravery, and then returned to Leavenworth and persisted in remaining, notwithstanding his life was constantly threatened and in danger. He was subsequently murdered at his own house by a company of "law and order" men, or Territorial militia, under the command of Capt. Frederick S. Emery, simply for refusng to leave the town. On the 25th of May, 1855, R. R. Reese, (who had been elected by Missouri votes to the Territorial council,) presided at a meeting which adopted the following resolutions unanimously:

"*Resolved*, That we heartily endorse the action of the committee of citizens that shaved, tarred and feathered, rode on a rail and sold by a negro William Phillips, the moral perjurer.

"*Resolved*, That we return our thanks to the committee for faithfully performing the trust enjoined upon them by the Pro-Slavery party.

"*Resolved*, That in order to secure peace and harmony to the community, we now solemnly declare, that the Pro-Slavery party will stand firmly by and carry out the resolutions reported by the committee appointed for that purpose on the memorable 30th."

(See these resolutions, note 22; Gihon, p. 35; Kansas Affairs, pp. 963, 965, 970, 1026.)

Judge Lecompte eloquently addressed the above meeting.

NOTE 28.

"On the afternoon of December 6, 1855, three men, Thomas W. Barber, Robert F. Barber and Thomas M. Pierson, left Lawrence to proceed to their homes, about seven miles distant (west of Lawrence). They had progressed nearly four miles when they saw a party of from twelve to fifteen horsemen traveling the road leading from Lecompton to the Wakarusa camp. These were Pro-Slavery men, and among them were Gen. Richardson, commander of the Kansas militia; Judge S. G. Cato, of the Supreme Court of the Territory; John P. Wood, Probate Judge and Police Magistrate of Douglas county; Col. J. N. Burns, a lawyer, of Weston, Mo., and Maj. Geo. W. Clarke, U. S. agent for the Pottawatomie Indians.

"The Barbers, who were brothers, and Pierson, their brother-in-law, had just left the main road and taken a nearer path to the left. Upon perceiving this movement, Clarke and Burns put spurs to their horses and dashed across the prairie with the obvious intention to intercept them. The Barbers thereupon slackened their pace, when Clarke, getting within speaking distance, ordered them to halt, a summons which they immediately obeyed. Richardson, Cato and the remainder of Clarke's party continued in full sight and at but a short distance. Clarke, who is a thick set man, about five feet three inches high, exceedingly loquacious and consequential in his manners, and notorious for his violent opposition to the Free-State people, commenced interrogating the Barbers, demanding to know who they were, where they were from and where they were going, to all of which questions Thomas W. Barber made mild and truthful replies. Clarke then ordered them to turn their horses heads and go with him and Burns, which demand Barber refused; whereupon Clarke drew his pistol, and taking deliberate aim, fired at Thomas W. Barber (the ball entering his abdomen), Burns discharging his pistol at almost the same instant. Robert F. Barber then returned the shot, firing three times in rapid succession, without any effect. Pierson had with him a small revolver, but could not get it out. Thomas W. Barber was without arms of any description. The parties then separated, taking opposite directions and galloping their horses. They had proceeded but a short distance when Thomas W. Barber remarked to his brother, with a smile, 'That fellow has shot me,' and placed his hand against his side. Robert, perceiving that he had dropped the reins and was riding unsteadily, hastened to his assistance and attempted to support him, but in a little while he slipped from his saddle and fell to the ground. His brother and Pierson immediately dismounted, but Thomas was dead.

"Clarke boastingly declared, when he entered the Wakarusa camp, 'I have sent another d—d Abolitionist to hell.'" (Gihon, p. 65; Kansas Affairs, pp. 1121-1128.)

Brewerton, a regular correspondent of the New York *Herald*, says: "There are circumstances connected with the life and character of this man Barber which make his death more particularly to be deplored. Barber is spoken of as a quiet, unoffensive and amiable man, domestic and unexceptionable in his habits and deeply attached to his wife, to whom he had been married between nine and ten years. He was unarmed when he received the death wound, and on his way to his home. His wife, to whom he had written to inform her of his coming, was expecting him. She is said to have loved her husband with more than ordinary devotion. It was her habit when she saw him coming back from his work to leave the house and go forth to meet him on his way. If he failed to return at the time indicated she grew anxious, and if his stay was prolonged oftentimes passed the night in tears. When ill, she would hang over his bed with all the anxiety of a mother for her child. She would seem, too, to have had a presentiment of some impending evil; for after exhausting every argument to prevent her husband from going to join the Free-State forces, at Lawrence, she said: 'Oh! Thomas, if you should be shot, I should be all alone, indeed; remember, I have no child, nothing in the wide world to fill your place.' And this was their last parting. And when the tidings of his death came she burst forth: 'They have left me a poor, forsaken creature, to mourn all my days. Oh my husband! they have taken from me all that I hold dear; one that I loved better than I loved my own life.'" (War in Kansas, p. 330.)

The following is from the pen of Hannah Anderson Ropes, taken from one of a series of letters written from Lawrence to her mother in the East, in 1854-5. She is one of the most charming of Kansas writers, and in emotional literature has few equals in the world. She says: "I believe I have forgotten to tell you that the funeral of Mr. Barber was deferred on account of the important business this week to be attended to. Another week has closed, and the Sabbath calls all people out to pay the last tribute of respect to poor Barber's memory. A December day, but clear, cloudless, dreadfully bright and windy, . . . yet the whole neighborhood seems astir with people picking their way to one center — the hotel — where not as last Monday evening for rejoicing they came together, but to mourn with the sufferers of a great sorrow: a widow made so by violence wholly unprovoked; a brother bereaved in a manner never to be forgotten, never to be thought of in years to come but with the smartest twinges of pain. The room we enter is a long dining hall. The walls are of limestone, rough and unplastered. Seats of plank stretch in rows closely packed through the whole length, with the exception of a narrow space for the clergyman. The seats are all filled. The atmosphere of the assembly is of the truest sympathy. Each soul seems personally aggrieved and afflicted. Silence is the only and most emphatic expression given to this grief. The first break upon that silence is the tread of many feet, and a smothered, broken sob that will not be wholly choked down. Working his way through the crowd appears a tall man with white hair, large blue eyes, and a very benevolent countenance. You see at once that he is a Methodist. He has clinging to his arm a small veiled figure. Every one knows 't is a widow, 'a widow indeed!' Then comes another sob, as she is borne along to the far end of the hall. The man of white hair stoops over her tenderly and whispers words of peace to her. I do not hear them; she does not. Now she sinks into a seat. A hymn is read and the crowd sing the tune 'Martin Luther,' so familiar to everybody, and stretching back over the whole length of the oldest life present. What a relief it is! How it gathers up and rolls away the pent-up emotions of the multitude! Now the white head sinks down over bended knees to the floor, and his voice utters its prayers and supplications, while the tears course down the cheeks of the speaker and his audience. The sobs of the broken heart grow fainter. Does she find a relief through the channels of other hearts? I believe so. Then follow short speeches from Col. Lane and Gen. Robinson, and a sad sermon from the white head. All the exercises are remarkably good of the kind. . . .

"The services are over and the people form a procession; men, with arms reversed, take the lead; then the body and its friends; then the whole crowd, mounted in carts drawn by oxen, wagons led by mules, and carriages of every pattern form into a solid line stretching far along the open country. Up over Mount Pleasant curves the road to the ground appropriated for a burial place, two miles away. What a sight it is! One like it could hardly be got up anywhere else, or under any other circumstances. This grand old country, venerable with its lofty trees, its smoothly-terraced hills, its serene repose, where the moccasin has only trod as at home and crept away in by places to take the sleep of d a h! The tread of the white man is fresh and new, but to-day the grand old prairie witnesses the burial of its second martyr! Now the soldiers make a wall on either side, with lifted hats, for the mourners to pass through. Gently the coffin is lowered to its last rest, while the words: 'Dust to dust,' 'I am the resurrection and the life,' are broken by the wailing wind and lost to the ears of the audience by the fast-coming sobs of that forlorn, childless, earth-stricken widow! The soldiers now approach; the audience and friends fall back, giving place to them while standing about the grave. At the signal of their commander, Uncle Jeff, one division after another bury the contents of their rifles in the last resting place of their much beloved and honored comrade." (Six Months in Kansas, pp. 146, 149.)

"Lay him down in hope and faith,
And above the broken sod
Once again to Freedom's God
Pledge yourself for life or death.

Historic Notes. 173

That the State whose walls ye lay
In your blood and tears to-day
Shall be free from bonds of shame,
And your goodly land untrod
By the feet of slavery, shod
With cursing and with flame."— *Whittier.*

NOTE 29.

Andrew H. Reeder, the first Governor of Kansas, was a resident of Easton, Pennsylvania. He was appointed to this high office by President Pierce, because of his eminent qualifications and his great influence in the Democratic party. He received his appointment in June, 1854, but did not arrive in Kansas until October. This, the first office he had ever accepted, was without his own solicitation; he was therefore prepared to execute the high trust, in justice and fairness to the settlers, in accordance to law and the principles of the Democratic party as he understood them. He came to Kansas a Douglas Democrat, and in less than a year was removed from office, because he dared to do right. The crimes and frauds which he saw committed on Kansas soil by the Pro-Slavery party so highly incensed him that he forever quit its ranks, and in May, 1856, he escaped from the Territory a Republican. When the civil war came on he and Nathaniel Lyon were the two first brigadier generals of the regular army appointed by Abrah m Lincoln. Reeder did not accept; his three sons, however, enlisted in the Union army. He died July 5th, 1864, at his home. I now give a brief account of his escape from Kansas:

On the seventh day of May, 1856, while he was examining witnesses at Tecumseh, before the Congressional committee on Kansas affairs, James F. Legate, who was a member of the grand jury, came and informed him that a plan to paralyze the Free-State party had been laid and was about to be carried out, by indicting all the officers of the provisional State government and judges of the election. A number of indictments had already been found, but as yet not passed. The grand jury at Lecompton, having been charged by Chief Justice Lecompte that the above officers were indictable, they voted by a large majority of the sixteen present, and without any testimony at all, to find true bills against Governor Robinson and Andrew H. Reeder for treason. The plotters of this crime knowing that on a warrant for treason they would not go to Lecompton, the court tried the strategy of a subpœna, but Reeder, seeing that it was irregular in form, disobeyed. On the eighth, the committee went to Lawrence to take testimony, when at about 2 o'clock P. M. a Mr. Fain, fresh from Georgia, who was acting as deputy marshal, came into the room of the committee with his posse, all armed, and served an attachment on Governor Reeder; whereupon Reeder put himself on his privilege, and asked that the committee protect him in it. This they refused to do, but Howard and Sherman clearly and decidedly gave their opinion that he was privileged from any such process for his arrest; Oliver holding the contrary. Reeder then stood upon his own defense and refused to obey, telling the deputy marshal that if he tried to arrest him, it would be at his peril. The posse then left.

Reeder then wrote to Governor Shannon and Judge Lecompte, stating that if they would give him their guaranty of personal safety and immediate return to the committee, he would go to Lecompton and testify. The next day Lecompte returned word that he had no answer to give.

Mr. Howard, the chairman of the Congressional committee, with Lowrey, Jenkins, Hutchinson, Roberts and others, then insisted that Reeder should leave the Territory, and not put his life in jeopardy any longer. Accordingly, on the night of the 10th of May he left with Jenkins, in a two-horse buggy, taking the road to Kansas City by way of Blanton's, on the Wakarusa, instead of going by Franklin, where the enemy was encamped. On the night of the 11th he arrived at the Eldridge hotel, in Kansas City, where he remained concealed eleven days. During this time he tried, through his friends, to find a safe passage down the river on a steamer, and failed. On the night of the 22d he disguised himself in the garb and demeanor of an Irishman, and boldly left his room, passed down the hall stairs, elbowed his way through a border ruffian crowd, and reached the front of the hotel, where he lazily stretched himself, and unchallenged took a seat near the front steps. Presently he got up and leisurely walked down the road, and went to the house of a Mr. Brown, quite out of town. All day the 23d he kept concealed in Brown's house.

Here Reeder determined to take a skiff and row down the river, and await the steamboat "J. M. Converse," Captain Bowman, for Pittsburg, knowing him to be friendly. The procuring of the skiff was left to —— Adams, and when it was quite dark he took aboard his charge, provided with bundles and two axes. They then dropped down half a mile below Randolph Landing, which is five miles from Kansas City, and fastening the skiff, went into the woods and slept till morning. On the afternoon of this day (the 24th) the "Converse" stopped at the landing, and as soon as the gang plank was run out, Reeder, with his bundle and axe on his shoulder, hot and puffing and blowing, went on board. Here he remained with the deck hands two days, and at last was landed, amid thunder and lightning, at a wood pile on the north bank of the Missouri. Here two companions, Bassett and Brackett, accompanied him across to the Mississippi, which they reached fifteen miles above Alton, at 8 o'clock A. M. on the 25th. Thus he effected his escape from the Territory, and perhaps from death. (Diary of Gov. A. H. Reeder.)

While Governor Reeder was thus secretly effecting his escape, no greater eventful days were crowded into Kansas history. Lawrence was sacked; the Eldridge hotel burned; the *Herald of Freedom* and *Kansas Free State* offices were destroyed, and the type thrown into the Kansas river; Governor Robinson and many others were arrested for treason; Charles Sumner was struck down in the United States Senate for his great speech, "The Crime Against Kansas;" Jones and Stewart were shot while in a defenseless condition, near Lawrence, for no other crime than that they were Free-State men; and John Brown struck his retributive blow on the Pottawatomie. And all this in less than six days—from the 19th to the 24th of May, 1856.

NOTE 30.

"The South Carolina flag was blood red, with a lone white star, and bore the inscription, 'Southern Rights.' This, at the sacking of Lawrence, on the 20th of May, 1856, was first hoisted over the *Herald of Freedom* office, and then removed to the Eldridge hotel, and there floated while the bombardment was going on." (Mrs. Robinson's "Kansas," p. 245.)

NOTE 31.

The calling out of the troops came about in this way: Sheriff Jones sent the following dispatch to Governor Shannon —

DOUGLAS COUNTY, K. T., Nov. 27, 1855.

SIR — Last night I, with a posse of ten men, arrested one Jacob Bronsom, by virtue of a peace warrant regularly issued, who on our return was rescued by a party of forty armed men, who rushed upon us suddenly from behind a house upon the roadside, all armed to the teeth with Sharpe's rifles.

You may consider an open rebellion as having already commenced, and I call upon you for 3,000 men to carry out the laws. Mr. Hargis, the bearer of this letter, will give you more particularly the circumstances.

Most respectfully,   SAMUEL J. JONES,
Sheriff of Douglas County.
His excellency WILSON SHANNON,
Governor Kansas Territory.

After a preliminary recital of the information obtained, Governor Shannon commands Maj. Gen. William P. Donaldson as follows:

You are hereby ordered to collect together as large a force as you can in your division and repair without delay to Lecompton, and report yourself to S. J. Jones, Sheriff of Douglas county. You will inform him of the number of men under your control, and render him all the assistance in your power should he require your aid in the execution of any legal process in his hands. The forces under your command are to be used for the sole purpose of aiding the sheriff in executing the law, and for none other.

I have the honor to be, your obedient servant,
WILSON SHANNON.

This struggle was temporarily held in abeyance by the treaty of Shannon, Lane and Robinson, which was executed December

8, 1855. At last, however, in the May following, the blast of deadly war was blown.

It may be well, in this connection, to give Sheriff Jones' opinion of Governor Shannon. Nine days after the above executive order, G. W. Clarke killed Thomas W. Barber, and two days after this killing the famous Shannon, Lane and Robinson treaty was signed, and Jones was foiled in his nefarious designs.

"Jones said if Shannon had n't been a d—d old fool, that peace would never have been declared. He (Jones) would have wiped Lawrence out. He had men and means enough to do it. He said if Sam. Wood ever came back to the Territory he would take him, or die in the attempt. He said he would issue his own proclamation, and not call upon Shannon, and he would raise boys enough in Missouri to blow Lawrence and every other d—d Abolition town to h—l. He would n't have any old grannies to stop him." (Harrison Nichols' testimony, Kansas Affairs, p. 1127.)

NOTE 32.

On the 20th day of May, 1856, Lawrence was taken by the chivalry of the South. The *Free State* press and *Herald of Freedom* and the Eldridge hotel were destroyed.

Gen. D. R. Atchison addressed the crowd who did the work as follows:

"Boys, this day I am a Kickapoo Ranger, by G—d. This day we have entered Lawrence with 'Southern Rights' inscribed upon our banner, and not one d—d Abolitionist dared to fire a gun. Now, boys, this is the happiest day of my life. We have entered that d—d town and taught the d—d Abolitionists a Southern lesson that they will remember until the day they die. And now, boys, we will go in again with our highly honorable Jones and test the strength of that d—d Free-State hotel, and teach the Emigrant Aid Company that Kansas shall be ours. Boys, ladies should and I hope will be respected by every gentleman. But when a woman takes upon herself the garb of a soldier by carrying a Sharpe's rifle, then she is no longer worthy of respect; trample her under your feet as you would a snake. Come on, boys! Now do your duty to yourselves and your Southern friends. Your duty I know you will do. If one man or woman dare stand before you, blow them to h—l with a chunk of cold lead." (Mrs. Robinson's, "Kansas," p. 243.)

NOTE 33.

"As to the charge of party bias, Lecompte says: 'I am proud of mine. It has from my first manhood to this day placed me in the ranks of the Democratic party. It has taught me to regard that party as the one *par excellence*, to which the destinies of this country are particularly intrusted for preservation. If it be intended to reach beyond that general application, and to charge a Pro-Slavery bias, I am proud, too, of this. I am the steady friend of Southern rights, under the constitution of the United States. I have been reared where slavery was recognized by the constitution of my State. I love the institution, as entwining itself around all my early and late associations.'" (Gihon, p. 165.)

NOTE 34.

Treasonable nuisance.

NOTE 35.

The Lecompton *Union* gave the following account of this affair:

"During this time appeals were made to Sheriff Jones to save the Aid Society's hotel. This news reached the company's ears, and was received with one universal cry of 'No! no! blow it up! blow it up!'

"About this time a banner was seen fluttering in the breeze over the office of the *Herald of Freedom*. Its color was a blood red, with a lone star in the center, and 'South Carolina' above. This banner was placed there by the Carolinians, Messrs. Wright and a Mr. Cross. The effect was prodigious. One tremendous and long-continued shout burst from the ranks. Thus floated in triumph the banner of South Carolina, that single white star, so emblematic of her course in the early history of our sectional disturbances. When every other Southern State stood almost upon the verge of ceding its dearest rights to the North, Carolina stood boldly out, the firm and unwavering advocate of Southern institutions.

"Thus floated victoriously the first banner of Southern rights over the Abolition town of Lawrence, unfurled by the noble sons of Carolina, and every whip of its folds seemed a death stroke to Beecher propagandism and the fanatics of the East. O! that its red folds could have been seen by every Southern eye!

"Mr. Jones listened to many entreaties, and finally replied that it was beyond his power to do anything, and gave the occupants so long to remove all property from it. He ordered two companies into each printing office to destroy the presses. Both presses were broken up and thrown into the street, the type thrown into the river, and all the material belonging to each office destroyed. After this was accomplished, and the private property removed from the hotel by different companies, the cannon were brought in front of the house, and directed their destructive blows upon the walls. The building caught on fire, and soon its walls came with a crash to the ground. *Thus fell the Abolition fortress;* and we hope this will teach the Aid Society a good lesson for the future." (Quoted by Gihon, p. 84.)

"Jones himself was in ecstacies. He sat upon his horse, contemplating the havoc he was making, and, rubbing his hands with wild delight, exclaimed: 'This is the happiest day of my life. I determined to make the fanatics bow before me in the dust and kiss the Territorial laws, and I have done it; by G—d, I have done it.'" (Gihon, p. 85.)

NOTE 36.

The Quantrell raid.

NOTE 37.

On the 19th and 20th of May, 1856, Charles Sumner made, in the U. S. Senate, his great speech—"*The crime against Kansas.*" In this he said: "A few short months have passed since this spacious mediterranean country was open only to the savage, who ran wild in its woods and prairies; and now it has already drawn to its bosom a population of freemen larger than Athens crowded within her historic gates, when her sons under Miltiades won liberty for mankind on the field of Marathon; more than Sparta contained when she ruled Greece, and sent forth her devoted children quickened by a mother's benediction to return with their shields or on them; more than Rome gathered on her seven hills, when under her kings she commenced that sovereign sway which afterward embraced the whole earth; more than London held when on the fields of Crecy and Agincourt the English banner was carried victoriously over the chivalrous hosts of France."

NOTE 38.

Mrs. H. A. Ropes gives the following pen portrait of Reese P. Brown, murdered on the 19th of January, 1856:

"Captain Brown lived but a few hours after his wounds were inflicted. He was taken prisoner by men from Platte county, and confined in a room, to be hung the next morning, but so greedy were his captors for his blood that, before he was really led out of the entrance to his prison, hatchets were raised above his head and bowie knives thrust into his body. He fell most barbarously wounded. At his earnest request he was placed in a wagon and taken to his home, where, on his arrival, he had just time enough to bid farewell to his wife and children.

"Captain Brown was born at the South, emigrated from Ohio to this Territory with his family, and located near Fort Leavenworth. In the autumn he came to Lawrence and remained till our safety was no longer in jeopardy. In personal appearance he was quite a marked man, even in a crowd. He was unusually tall, with a rich brown complexion, dark, abundant hair and beard, and eyes large, dark, and sad in expression. I do not think that any one who ever saw him will forget his personal appearance; and no dweller in Kansas can ever forget the mark his cruel death has made upon the pages of its early history." (Six Months in Kansas, p. 169.)

NOTE 39.

"On Monday, May 19th, word came into Lawrence of the murder of a young man by the name of Jones, the support of his widowed mother. He had been to Lawrence for a bag of meal, and returning, was ordered to halt by a band of the marshal's posse near Blanton's bridge. He obeyed the order of the ruffianly assassins, and they disarmed him. Then they ordered him to proceed, and, as he did so, two of the posse exclaimed: 'Let's shoot the d—d Abolitionist!' Suiting the action to the word, the balls sped on their swift errand, and the recording angel wrote against the names of some high in power another murder.

"Several young men immediately left Lawrence to go to the spot where young Jones fell, and about a mile from Lawrence they met two men from Westport. Another ball did the bidding of the slave interest, and another witness appeared against its supporters in the high court where perjury enters not, and packed juries are unknown. The body of young Stewart, so lately come among us, was brought into town and laid in the hotel. So sudden was his passage from this to the unseen life, that the placid countenance wore not the aspect of death, but the beautiful repose of a dreamy sleep." (Mrs. Robinson's "Kansas," p. 238.)

NOTE 40.

During Monroe's administration the Missouri compromise measure came up. A bill organizing the Territory of Missouri was introduced, and James Tallmadge, of New York, moved in the House to insert a clause prohibiting any further introduction of slaves, and freeing those already there on attaining the age of twenty-five years. This came to a vote, standing eighty-seven for, to seventy-six against. Afterward, on a bill to organize the Territory of Arkansas, on a motion to exclude slavery from any Territory of the United States north of latitude 36° 30′, Mr. Cobb, of Georgia, looking at Tallmadge, said: "A fire has been kindled which all the waters of the ocean cannot put out, and which only seas of blood can extinguish." Tallmadge replied: "If dissolution of the Union must take place, let it be so. If civil war must come, let it come. My hold on life is probably as frail as any man's who hears me; but while it lasts it shall be devoted to the freedom of man. If blood is necessary to put out this fire, I shall not hesitate to give my own."

NOTE 41.

"John Brown was a Bible worshiper, if ever any man was. He read and meditated on the Bible constantly. In his will he bequeathed a Bible to each of his childen and grandchildren, and he wrote to his family a few days before his execution: 'I beseech you every one to make the Bible your daily and nightly study.'" (Sanborn's "Life of John Brown," p. 121.)

NOTE 42.

"'The weapons used were short cutlasses or artillery sabres which had been originally worn by a military company in Ohio, and were brought from Akron, in 1855, by John Brown. They were straight and broad, like an old army sword, and were freshly ground for this expedition at the camp of John Brown, jr." (Sanborn's "John Brown," p. 264.)

NOTE 43.

At the time of this "taking off" by John Brown, Governor Robinson, Gaius Jenkins, G. W. Brown, G. W. Deitzler and G. W. Smith were under arrest and indictment for high treason, and it is highly probable they would have been hanged for the crime charged had not this retributive blow been struck by John Brown just at this time. Lecompte, the Chief Justice, was just the man who would have gloried in executing sentence. But John Brown, who took in the whole situation of Kansas affairs, and saw the wrath of the slave power culminating in the blood of freemen, arose like some avenging spirit, with a genius quickened by inspiration, and struck the blow which sent terror into the soul of Lecompte, and paralyzed the judicial arm. Brown afterward said: "If the Lord had delivered Judge Lecompte into my hands, it would have required the Lord to have taken him out again."

NOTE 44.

"Fugit is the person who made a bet in this (Leavenworth) city last August, 1856, that before night he would have a Yankee scalp. He got a horse and rode out into the country and met a German, a brother-in-law of the Rev. E. Nute, named Hoppe. He asked if he was from Lawrence; Hoppe replied that he was. Fugit immediately leveled his revolver and fired, the shot taking effect in the temples, and Hoppe fell a corpse. The assassin dismounted from his horse, cut the scalp from the back of his head, *tied it to the end of a pole*, and returned to town, exhibiting it to the people and boasting of his exploit. The body of the victim was found shortly after and buried on Pilot Knob, about two miles distant from the city. This same Fugit was one of the party who, when the widow came from Lawrence to look for her husband's corpse, forced her on board a steamer and sent her down the river. A gentleman now living in this city (Leavenworth) saw him exhibiting four scalps at one time during the troubles of last summer" (1856). (Correspondent of *Missouri Democrat*, quoted by Gihon, p. 300.)

NOTE 45.

"When the army from Missouri was disbanded, by order of Gov. Geary, on the morning of the 15th of November, 1856, the great body of it returned at once to the State by the Westport road, committing every atrocity in their power as they passed along. They burned the saw mill at Franklin, stole a number of horses, and drove off all the cattle they could find.

A detachment calling themselves the 'Kickapoo rangers,' numbering about 250 or 300 men, under command of Col. Clarkson, took the road for Lecompton, where they forded the river early in the afternoon on their way to the northern part of the Territory. This party was mounted and well armed, and looked like as desperate a set of ruffians as ever were gathered together. They still carried the black flag; and their cannon, guns, swords and carriages were yet decorated with the black emblems of their murderous intentions.

"Six men of this detachment, when within a few miles of Lecompton, halted by a field, where a poor, inoffensive lame man named David C. Buffum was at work. They entered the field, and after robbing him of his horses one of them shot him in the abdomen, from which wound he soon afterward died. The murderer also carried away a pony belonging to a young girl." (Gihon, p. 166.)

For this crime one Charles Hays was arrested, indicted for murder in the first degree, and set at liberty without trial by Chief Justice Lecompte. He was then arrested by order of Governor Geary, and again set at liberty by Lecompte. And this ended the conflict between the executive and the judiciary of the Territory.

NOTE 46.

Capt. Samuel Walker went twice with his small army to Lecompton. First, on the 16th of August, 1856, at which time the fort of Titus was taken and burned, and five prisoners liberated. The second time was about three weeks after, which was shotless and bloodless. The prisoners were all liberated, and Lecompton fell.

NOTE 47.

"On Monday morning, February 9, 1857, accompanied by Dr. Gihon and Richard McAllister, Esq., the Governor visited successively the Supreme Court, the Council and the House of Representatives, all of which were in session. As they passed into the latter hall and took their seats within the bar and among the members, Sherrard, who occupied a seat in one corner of the room, unseen by the Governor, was observed to manifest a strange uneasiness of manner, and with a heavy scowl upon his countenance, and muttering some unintelligible words, suddenly arose and quit the apartment. The Governor remained a half hour or more, and then took his leave. As he was about to step from the main hall into the adjoining anteroom, Sherrard stood in the door, having gone off and procured an extra pistol to the one he usually wore, both of which, contrary to his custom, he had placed conveniently in a belt buckled on the outside of his clothing. In his breast he also carried a huge bowie knife. Before the Governor had closed the door, Sherrard accosted him with the words: 'You have treated me like a d—d scoundrel.' The Governor passed on without noticing the man, much less his opprobrious salutation. Mr. McAllister followed, and as they passed toward the outer door his person interposed between that of Sherrard and the Governor. Dr. Gihon was the last to leave the hall and enter the anteroom, when he saw Sherrard spitting after the Governor, at the same time muttering oaths and threats of defiance, his right hand firmly grasping one of the pistols in his belt. Adjoining the anteroom was another small room, the door of which was partially opened, and there stood several ruffians who had been apprised of the intended assassination, and were ready to take their part in the bloody work. The Governor and his friends were unarmed. Had he halted to speak to Sherrard, or turned upon him, or in any possible way given an excuse for the deed, he would have been shot down like a dog, and himself and companions riddled with balls, and the murderer's allies would have been left to tell the story and justify their infamous crime." (Gihon, pp. 233, 234.)

NOTE 48.

The same G. W. Clarke who shot Barber went through Linn county in the fall of 1856, at the head of a band of Pro-Slavery cut throats, outlaws and ruffians, and devastated the county with fire and sword. They burned a store at Sugar

Mound, and other buildings near the present town of Mound City; they pillaged from and drove out the Free-State settlers along Little and Big Sugar, and threatened death to all who should come back. In the following winter Montgomery organized his band, styled the 'Self-Protective Company,' afterwards known by the immortal name of *Jayhawkers*. By this move of Montgomery's, which was strictly retaliatory, the Free-State men soon returned, and ever after stood by their claims and defended their rights. A writer, now of Topeka, and who in the saddle was one of Montgomery's men in 1858, then wrote as follows: "Montgomery, from his retirement, saw it all. He saw every Free-State man of note either driven from or harrassed into leaving the county. He saw them deliberately plundered of cattle, horses, goods and crops; in many instances their cabins burned, and outrages committed of such atrocity that even decency forbids their mention. He saw the guilty parties grow rich in a night on property thus pillaged from his Free-State neighbors. He saw all attempts at redress by law scouted at or thwarted.

"For a long time Montgomery and others waited for redress by law of all their abuses, and probably would have waited longer, had they seen any signs of justice assuming the scepter of command; but things daily continuing to grow worse, he at last obeyed the call of an injured people, and summoning a few of his neighbors together, he enrolled them in a company styled the 'Self-Protective Company,' and took the field to check some of the gigantic evils that had crept into the politic and legal code of the county. A policy of action was then agreed upon, which was strictly carried out. Every man of influence in Linn county, who sustained the 'Blue Lodge' in its secret machinations, and upheld the 'Bogus Code' and the Pro-Slavery Lecompton government, whether by fraud, violence or murder, was warned to leave the Territory in a certain time, and take with him his property. Some left, and some refused to go. Those who did not leave within the specified time were visited again, when their houses were searched, and arms, ammunition, horses, etc., taken from them. In no case, however, was the house of a Pro-Slavery man burned, or his property wantonly destroyed, by Montgomery and his men. The ejected occupant had full permission to sell or transfer his property in any way he chose, no restraint whatever being imposed on his actions.

"This bold and decided course on the part of the Free-State men had the desired effect; peace was for the time being secured, and Montgomery retired to his home. So universally approved of, however, was his course, by the settlers from whose neck he had lifted the galling yoke they had so long worn, that they would have at any time responded *en masse* to any call he might have made on their time and services." (W. P. Tomlinson's "Kansas in 1858.")

NOTE 49.

The "Bogus Laws" were publicly burned in some parts of Linn in 1855 and 1856.

NOTE 50.

These were slavery phrases of the border ruffian days.

NOTE 51.

A Sharpe's rifle was in those days called a "Beecher," in honor of Henry Ward Beecher.

NOTE 52.

JOHN BROWN'S PARALLELS.

While the following letter is dated at the Trading Post, in Linn county, it was actually written on the Pottawatomie, while John Brown was leisurely and carefully wending his way to Canada with his captured colored people, there to set them free. The letter was addressed to the New York *Tribune:*

TRADING POST, KAS., January, 1859.

GENTLEMEN: You will greatly oblige an humble friend by allowing the use of your columns while I briefly state two parallels in my poor way.

Not one year ago eleven quiet citizens of this neighborhood, William Robertson, William Colpetzer, Amos Hall, Austin Hall, John Campbell, Asa Snyder, Thomas Stillwell, William Hairgrove, Asa Hairgrove, Patrick Ross and B. L. Reed were gathered up from their work and their homes by an armed force, under one Hamilton, and, without trial or opportunity to speak in their own defense, were formed into line, and all but one shot, five killed and five wounded; one fell unharmed, pretending to be dead. All were left for dead. The only crime alleged against them was that of being Free-State men. Now, I inquire what action has ever since the occurrence in May last been taken by either the President of the United States, the Governor of Missouri, the Governor of Kansas, or any of their tools, or by any Pro-Slavery or administration man, to ferret out and punish the perpetrators of this crime?

Now for the other parallel: On Sunday, December 19th, a negro man called Jim came over to the Osage settlement from Missouri, and stated that he, together with his wife, two children and another negro man were to be sold within a day or two, and begged for help to get away. On Monday (the following) night, two small companies were made up to go to Missouri and forcibly liberate the five slaves, together with other slaves. One of these companies I assumed to direct. We proceeded to the place, surrounded the buildings, liberated the slaves, and also took certain property supposed to belong to the estate. We, however, learned before leaving that a portion of these articles we had taken belonged to a man living on the plantation as a tenant, and who was supposed to have no interest in the estate. We promptly returned to him all we had taken. We then went to another plantation, where we found five more slaves, took some property, and two white men. We moved all slowly away into the Territory for some distance, and then sent the white men back, telling them to follow us as soon as they chose to do so. The other company freed one female slave, took some property, and, as I am informed, killed one white man, the master, who fought against the liberation.

Now for a comparison: Eleven persons are forcibly restored to their natural and inalienable rights, with but one man killed, and all hell is stirred from beneath. It is currently reported that the Governor of Missouri has made a requisition upon the Governor of Kansas for the delivery of all such as were concerned in the last-named "dreadful outrage." The marshal of Kansas is said to be collecting a posse of Missouri (not Kansas) men at West Point, in Missouri, a little town about ten miles distant, to enforce the laws; all Pro-Slavery, conservative, Free-State and dough-face men, and administration tools, are filled with holy horror.

Consider the two cases, and the action of the administration party.   Respectfully yours,   JOHN BROWN.

NOTE 53.

"Kansas furnished more troops to the Union army in proportion to her inhabitants than any other State in the Union, her population in 1860 being 107,206, and troops furnished 20,151."

www.ingramcontent.com/pod-product-compliance
Lightning Source LLC
Chambersburg PA
CBHW020932230426
43666CB00008B/1653